IDENTITY AND IDEOLOGY

Recent Titles in
Contributions to the Study of Education

IDENTITY AND IDEOLOGY

Sociocultural Theories of Schooling

STANLEY WILLIAM ROTHSTEIN

Contributions to the Study of Education, Number 49

Greenwood Press
New York • Westport, Connecticut • London

Library of Congress Cataloging-in-Publication Data

Rothstein, Stanley William.
   Identity and ideology : sociocultural theories of schooling /
Stanley William Rothstein.
      p.   cm.—(Contributions to the study of education, ISSN
0196-707X ; no. 49)
   Includes bibliographical references (p.) and index.
   ISBN 0-313-27744-3 (alk. paper)
      1. Educational sociology—United States. 2. Educational
sociology—Europe. 3. Capitalism—United States. 4. Capitalism—
Europe.   I. Title.   II. Series.
LC191.4.R68   1991
370.19—dc20   91-22987

British Library Cataloguing in Publication Data is available.

Library of Congress Catalog Card Number: 91-22987
ISBN: 0-313-27744-3
ISSN: 0196-707X

First published in 1991

Greenwood Press, 88 Post Road West, Westport, CT 06881
An imprint of Greenwood Publishing Group, Inc.

Printed in the United States of America

The paper used in this book complies with the
Permanent Paper Standard issued by the National
Information Standards Organization (Z39.48-1984).

10 9 8 7 6 5 4 3 2 1

Contents

Preface

This book discusses the relationships between capitalism and schooling, paying special attention to European and American systems. Capitalism, since its birth, has been a development of European nations; in other areas of the world it came later and involved imitation.

In order for capitalism to work, it must bring workers out of their homes and into factories and offices; it must commoditize their labor power. To do this is to make labor a cost of production, subject to the laws of the free market. Labor becomes another commodity that must be brought together and exploited. Inexpensive labor costs are a practical goal for capitalists, who must compete with one another for scarce resources and customers.

From this we can see that the schools that capitalism establishes have a primary interest: the development of an ideology and culture that make it natural for students to accept proletarianization. This method is superior to the use of force because the control that comes to be utilized is a symbolic one. To the degree that students internalize this educational training, the system is able to maintain itself and the property relations that sustain it. Therefore, the good student is one who accepts the ideology of schools and the status quo in economic and social life.

This book seeks to uncover relationships between educational systems and other structures in society. It traces the roles of schooling and the family in establishing the identities of individuals at work and in their private lives. Further, it grapples with the "how-to" of these reproductive agencies by studying the ideological effects and linguistic constructions they use to influence the identity, knowledge, and thought of individuals. Today it is of vital importance that we understand what educational systems are trying to achieve and how they go about their work. If they are permitted to define themselves as they have in the past, the difficulty of upgrading or reforming them will increase beyond calculation. Indeed, the persistence of democracy in the United States depends, in part, upon whether its educational system can break away from its preoccupation with the demands of capitalism and move toward more democratic perspectives.

Acknowledgments

To some, the materials in this book may seem overly simplified. Certain chapters—those on the social relations of production, for instance—may appear uneven in their level of sophistication. It is the writer's opinion, however, that the philosophical and abstract ideas presented here need to find a wider audience.

It is my intention that the book be of interest not only to specialists in the areas of social philosophy, sociology, and psychoanalysis but also to other people who are interested in schooling and the way human identity is formed in capitalist systems.

From the nature of such an undertaking one feels a need to express one's gratitude toward the many friends who helped and supported this effort. For continuous friendship and support, I should like particularly to thank my colleagues, Professors Walter F. Beckman, J. Kenneth Preble, Louise Adler, and William Callison. For long-term intellectual dueling and friendship, I should like to express my debt to Professor Emeritus Conrad Briner of Claremont Graduate School. For the time made available to me through a sabbatical leave from California State University, Fullerton, I want to thank Professor Mary Kay Tetrault, Dean of the School of Human Development and Community Services.

Finally, I want to thank Sue and Stacy, my wife and daughter, for their love, understanding, and friendship. Of course I alone am responsible for the ways materials were analyzed and presented in this book.

IDENTITY AND IDEOLOGY

1

Sociocultural Theories of Schooling: An Introduction

Educational systems cannot be defined apart from their practices. These are governed by inculcation and pedagogic control and by the needs of the state that sponsors them. Schooling can do no more than consolidate the centralization of state and educational power, developing a systematic, total control over the personal and educational lives of teachers and students. Hence to think of schools as centers of instruction and rationalism is to ignore their ideological basis. Educational systems cannot exist in a vacuum, for they are interdependent institutions that must reproduce the social relations of production generation after generation. Because our interest is in an understanding of how this is done, how students become "educated" persons, our focus will be multidisciplinary in its approach. We will use the perspectives of many social science disciplines to learn how schools transform students' minds into right-thinking, obedient, law-abiding citizens and workers.

To begin, this transformation commences at birth, when neonates are subjected to a continuing barrage of pedagogical acts from parents and other significant adults. These teachings provide the children with a mastery of signification codes and linguistic categories that contain the class identity and folklore of relatives and kinfolk. They are crucial in transforming the children into social beings who are aware of their role in the family. Later, in schools, the children, come into contact with the arbitrary language, culture, and ideas of the educated classes in society; they learn their place in the educational and socioeconomic hierarchy. These, then, are the outcomes associated with the work commonly referred to as teaching. Teachers, acting as agents of the state and society, change youth into social beings and identities, who can then be used by other institutions and work agencies.

As our interest is in educational production, or the "how-to" of social and educational reproduction, some attention should be given to its structural components. A description of the invariant elements of pedagogic action can be deduced from the work of structural Marxists. These components can be combined in many ways and should be thought of as an ideal type, in the Weberian sense. They consist of:

1. the schoolteacher who does the actual work in the educational production process
2. the educational process itself, or the pedagogical actions used to produce and transmit knowledge to students
3. the student's ideas, thoughts, perceptions, and feelings after he or she has been transformed
4. the instruments used in the production of educational knowledge, or those materials, texts, buildings, and legal-rational organizations used to create the world of schooling for students and teachers
5. the higher levels of schooling or work that use educational knowledge for their own purposes.

These structural elements of educational production can be helpful in simplifying social interaction in classrooms. But they cannot be understood without placing them in the social, political, and economic configurations of historical events. They cannot be used without considering the social relations that accompany production in the economic sectors. This structuralist orientation can help us to compare schooling as it has evolved in different stages of human history. But it has the unfortunate tendency to isolate educational production from other spheres in capitalist systems. It relates educational production to its internal elements rather than to the symbolic and cultural controls of the larger society. Educational production is seen as a way of maintaining social cohesion, as a functionalist response to the need of social and educational reproduction. It regards its practices as immutable, something students must passively subject themselves to as a rite of passage. Educational production tends to see students in concrete, commonsense terms. The individual exists for the organization as a coded entity, and there is no doubt about the class, race, or sexual identification of a unique person, different from others who have come before. Yet this individual requires the same pedagogic training and discipline, the same schoolwork. These pedagogic actions teach students to accept the world as it is: families, schools, churches, governments, and economic systems are presented as unchangeable givens deserving blind acceptance and support.

Modern structural Marxists discounted the experiences of individuals. Louis Althusser developed theoretical understandings of the individual that were antihumanistic and antiempirical; the individual, as we shall see in chapter 4, was no longer seen as a subject in control of his or her life; this person's experiences could not be understood through empirical validations. Althusser insisted upon a strict separation between theory and practice. The historical and social reality of schools were to be subordinated to theoretical concepts and ideas; the pedagogic efforts of teachers were viewed as external aspects of the idea as it was revealed to individuals through their stream of consciousness. The actual experiences in classrooms were merely a world of appearances reflecting the imaginary social relations between teachers and students. Language and culture explained this school world to participants, giving it a sense of orderliness and rationality that it often did not possess. For Althusser, only abstract theoretical concepts, grounded in internal consistencies and logic, could provide insights into the complex social phenomena of educational production.[1] Bourdieu, on the other hand, began his study of educational systems by focusing on the pedagogic act as inculcation and the perpetration of symbolic violence on students.[2] From this, he developed an elaborate theory of pedagogic work and the ways pedagogic authority and control developed in educational systems. Both believed schools were essentially agencies of inculcation and reproduction. Yet they began by choosing different features of schooling as their basis of investigation. Althusser was more interested in society as an entity, whereas Bourdieu focused more on educational systems and their practices. Neither attempted to reduce everything to an economic explanation, although they did recognize its intrinsic importance. Both were concerned with the linguistic and cultural characteristics of educational systems and the economic conditions they sought to validate and reproduce.

The problems of studying educational systems in cross-disciplinary ways are formidable. Attempts to do so have been marked by some success and by significant failures and misunderstandings. The specific nature of an educational system can express itself in differing forms of curriculum, pedagogy, and evaluation practices, in differing forms of symbolic violence and control. But educational production will always express, in one way or another, the needs of the society that supports it. Of course, there will be some interplay of influence, with educational systems sometimes appearing to change or affect social and economic institutions. The products of education reflect the tension and conflicts that exist in society. What outcomes develop and how these change or sustain the social system can only be studied through theoretical analysis. Sociocultural theories attempt to provide explanatory ideas about educational production and its consumption.[3] They identify ideological influences, paying attention not only to classroom communications but also to the ways in which such messages are constructed so that they appear to be, in fact, true presentations of reality.

KNOWLEDGE AND IDEOLOGY

Thinking of education as a productive process allows us to speak of the ways educational knowledge is transmitted to students. Here, ideologies play a significant role, providing rationales for many educational practices and outcomes. Social philosophers have linked ideology to the individual's inability to understand his or her position inside the school or workplace. It is related to an individual's consciousness, to his or her ability to act as a subject who thinks, acts, and changes the world in which he or she lives. Both Althusser's and Bourdieu's theories of knowledge saw the individual as someone who could recognize himself only through ideological concepts and language. In their work, any recognition of one's position in school or society, or one's relations to the economic and social order, was necessarily an instance of misrecognition.

But Paul Hirst, critiquing Althusser's work, argued that such interpretations were not epistemological categories at all.[4] Ideology did not describe false or illusionary insights into the nature of an individual's condition in society. Its effects, regardless of the logic of its structure, were very real for persons who experienced them. Educational knowledge might be immersed in ideological thought, but it had its embodiment in the daily practices that occurred in classrooms and everyday life. It was a lived form of thought, maintaining close relationships with traditional forms of contemplation and practice. Its ideas were always determined by the experiences of individuals living and working together.

Still, there are difficulties in distinguishing whether certain thoughts are ideological or not. Traditionally, ideology has been used in a pejorative sense, to signify the falsity of a set of ideas or practices. But recently Althusser and Geuss have provided a more expansive definition.[5] Ideologies are produced by individuals living and working together, and there is no known instance of a social system that did not possess them. Each social stratum or class has its own ideological beliefs, but those who have more social or economic power often prevail. Therefore, we would be in error if we limited our discussion to families and schools alone. Ideologies can be found in many different forms, in almost every phase of social life. Althusser believed they were an essential, organic part of social systems, the medium through which lived experiences were interpreted and understood in everyday life.

If we accept that ideologies have always been with us, what need do they fulfill? Perhaps individuals need to think of themselves as the center of their existence, as free and independent persons who can act to control the world in which they live. Perhaps they need ideas that will help them to understand why they are here, how they should live their lives, and how they fit into the larger scheme of things.

Particular ideologies emanate from the class positions of individuals living and working together and depend upon the history and social relations of production that have evolved over time.[6] These include ideas, concepts, and memories that have grown out of class struggles and other important events in history. As Durkheim and others have shown, however, they also include many solidarity-building attitudes and beliefs that help to sustain social systems and the national and social identities of peoples.

The ideology of schooling provides both teacher and student with rationales that allow them to see themselves as the center of the schooling process. This ideological approach creates a problem for those who wish to study educational systems empirically. Some form of signification or language must be used by them to communicate and code data. But this transformation of social reality into language, signs, and linguistic categories is the essence of the ideological effect, distorting understandings of the production of educational knowledge as it occurs in state schools. The researcher who wants to struggle against these distortions must find some way of escaping this seemingly insoluble dilemma. One way is to present the study as a work in process rather than an attempted portrayal of social reality. Data can be understood as successive approximations, and the suppositions involved in the process of changing social interaction into language can be explored. The linguistic and sign systems of the schools are important social phenomena, as they are used to instruct students and to provide data for researchers. They introduce the reader to a world that is controlled and orderly, one in which human concepts are taken as universals not needing analysis or critical thought. Most empirical attempts to study schooling pay little attention to the processes of educational production and the ways in which language helps individuals to construct social situations. But the researcher who wants to go beyond empiricism needs to describe and demonstrate the production of the ideological effect in schooling's practices, thus showing the reader how subjects and the reader are being manipulated. More and more, a sophisticated study of schooling becomes an introspection, a discovering of the processes and effects of signification systems being used to shape the minds of teachers and the children they serve. Of course empirical forms of theory and research are still dominant in educational journals today. All efforts to school youth occur in massive state institutions, and all place limits on the levels of knowledge students can achieve in their schools and stratified colleges and universities. Ideologies are important for sociocultural theories because they attempt to reveal and make reasonable the educational knowledge made accessible to working-class and lower-middle class students. Yet these explanations are marred by distortions that hide the true nature of educational systems in modern society.

The teaching profession is portrayed as one which seeks to help children learn what they will need to know when they reach maturity. But its role in perpetuating the social relations of educational and economic production are seldom discussed or recognized by teachers or students. The traditional ideas that teachers disseminate reproduce the social relations of schools and society by normalizing them over the course of a student's educational career. Schooling can thus be seen as one of the most conservative institutions in every social system, and educators can be viewed as transmission agents once the veil of ideology is lifted. The practices associated with the production of educational knowledge in mass schools confirms the student's inferior status and condition inside the building. The student is, by definition, the person who does not know, who needs instruction. The knowledge students need to master is outside their minds and bodies and known only to their teachers, to the paid representatives of the state. The effects of this pedagogic work in classrooms is felt by teachers, too. They are the ones forced to maintain the state's agenda of inculcation. They force children to learn a curriculum, language, and culture alien to their daily needs and concerns. How is it possible to produce educational outcomes using a language and culture that only the dominant few possess? Is this, the center of the symbolic violence that Bourdieu talks about in chapter 3? And do these practices and ideological structures mean that the class struggle, which Marx made the center of his work, is taking place in educational systems today?

Althusser and Lacan dispute this idea that the individual is a subject who struggles against the life forms he encounters. They leave little room for individual or collective subjects who act upon the world in which they live. They see the pervasiveness and work of ideology as one which produces individuals who willingly or unconsciously accept their subjugation. The production of ideological or educational knowledge is also seen as something that happens without human beings who will and produce such products. If the individual is not capable of understanding social reality because of linguistic and cultural distortions, who is supposed to take part in the class struggle? According to Althusser and Lacan, the individual lives and works as though he were the determiner of his thoughts and actions, as if he really did exist as a separate and identifiable entity. But the outcomes of his work and his place in the social system are never those that he willed or intended, because in that case he would be a real subject and not an ''as if'' subject who was created by linguistic and cultural categories. This idea that the individual is not real, but merely a person who misperceives that he or she is real, borders on the absurd, even as it forces us to examine more closely the influence of language and culture on the identity of human beings in modern society.

For Althusser, this break with humanism is seen as the most important feature of Marx's more mature work. Before Marx, humanism was dominated by Descartes and his subject–object dialogue. The individual was a subject who acted, the Cartesian ego who created the physical and social order within which he lived. He was the subject who could reconstitute the object world into language and knowledge; he could know that world as it really existed. Althusser was one of the first to place these suppositions in doubt, to transform this individual as subject into an object created by language and culture. Now the individual is seen as a consequence of particular practices. The creation or production of subjects, as we know them in our everyday lives, is the work of ideology and ideological state apparatuses such as the family and the schools. The individual, in this new definition of the self in modern society, cannot go on assuming that the transposition of the object world into linguistic and cultural categories and understandings is knowledge of that world. Individuals in Althusser's sense do not make the world they live in. They are born into it. They learn to speak the language of their parents and others who lived before them, and they think the thoughts of these others throughout their lifetimes.[7] They have no part in making the world they live in, and even their own sense of themselves is little more than a recognition of linguistic categories that others have used to characterize them at the earliest moments in their lives.

Only now does the profound role of the family begin to appear. The work of preparing individuals for life in the schools and workplace falls to the family. Freud's studies of the unconscious, disorganized, irrational, and contradictory nature of the self attacked older ideas of the rational and controlled individual, or ego. Lacan's work, which is discussed in chapter 4, saw the period from birth to the Oedipal period as a crucial time during which the infant moved from nature to culture, language, and society. It was this process of linguistic and social development that constituted the child as subject. But the child's recognition of itself depended upon the way others perceived it. The child could only imagine what it was like, and its thoughts were colored by the ways others characterized it. This recognition of the linguistic categories others applied to him or her as an infant constituted a misrecognition of the self. The significant others who identified the child were part of a social order, adults who often accepted their places in that system with little thought or introspection. This process of misrecognition of oneself is the essence of ideological thought, awareness, behavior, and experience at home and later in schools. According to Althusser, it is this initial experience of misperception of one's identity that disqualifies one from playing any part in developing knowledge of oneself and the world later in life.

Students come to schools with their personal identities, learned in families and neighborhoods. These are real for them, no matter how illusionary they may seem to theoreticians. The process of providing youth with institutional identities is bound up with educational stratification and an awareness of class position as an important feature of schooling. Lacan may be wrong when he points to the Oedipal complex as the one and only stage when an individual can successfully resolve his or her problems. The self is always searching for itself, always being reconstituted by the family, the schools, and the workplace. Schooling experiences play their part in creating the world for students in the classroom. Traditional education provides a situation to which the teacher and student must adapt if they are to enter into the work of the classroom, if they are to give and receive pedagogic actions. And it is from this educational work that misrecognition occurs and the ideological effect is produced by linguistic and cultural understandings that rank students and sensitize them to their places in school and society.

Teachers are the agents of these socialization and selection processes. They have no other recourse than to use their available repertoire of language and signifying systems when they speak to their students. They must use what is familiar to them if they are to gain attention. But these linguistic and cultural understandings generate ideological insights and understandings about classroom life. The control teachers exercise over students is similar to that exercised by parents. It also has features that look very much like the way bosses react to workers. But it has its own ethical basis, its own history and culture, and it cannot be changed easily. The teachers who want to go beyond these practices will have to subvert their own curriculums. They will have to show students, over time, how what they are learning in books and through language is not a true reflection of reality but merely a distorted version of one particular social situation. This can be done by calling the students' attention to the suppositions that support the educational practices in the classroom. It can be done by making students more aware of the components of culture and the ways in which schooling's culture affects the students' attitudes, toward themselves and toward others with whom they come in contact. Whereas traditional teachers present materials without thinking of their own biases or those of the writers and publishers of the text being used, teachers who want to go beyond inculcation display materials and show how they provide an ideological effect that has as its primary purpose the manipulation of the individual's thoughts and perceptions. This makes the materials in the curriculum, and the signification systems used to convey them, the focus of attention and analysis. The message is that structures of the mind or imagination cannot reveal the real because they cannot encompass even the merest fraction of it. Linguistic categories can show how they were constructed even as they cannot reveal or verify knowledge about the schooling and working processes themselves. Whereas traditional teachers are closed to these ideas and to a recognition of the ways in which suppositions and language distort perceptions and understandings, progressive teachers are more open and concerned about ideological structures and their effects on the selves of students and their understandings of the world.

No pedagogical materials come into being without human beings choosing them. No books are authorless. All of them have men and women who have written the texts, who have seen the world in ways that need to be understood. There can be discussions about these texts, of course. There can be arguments about what they mean. But teachers are the final arbiters of such differences. They are the ones who can alert students to the ways in which certain books are chosen and others are not. They can make students more aware of subtle forms of censorship. They have the authority to declare competing interpretations to be more or less valid. But they have to be ready to take the heat from certain agents of the state and the economy. This is true wherever schooling exists.

To sum up: if we recognize that educational practice is the work of the state, we must also recognize that certain curriculum materials are too comprehensive in their content and thereby useless for learning more deeply about particular subjects. Such a curriculum loses its analytical value and tends to be too one-sided in its approach to ideas and social happenings that are experimental in nature, that challenge the status quo. Ideas that are more familiar to teachers and students tend to be more easily accepted and used in the classroom.

DISSOLVING THE PERSONAL EXPERIENCES OF INDIVIDUALS

Returning to the ideas of Lacan and Althusser, we are presented with important insights and problems. The notion that there are limits to what students can know in their schoolwork seems reasonable enough. The corollary that new forms of schooling would require an unmasking of curriculum and teaching methods follows logically. When teachers help students to see that curriculum and teaching practices are all part of the ideological effects that lie at the center of educational production, students (and teachers) can begin to see how their lives together are determined by outside forces they cannot see or fully understand. Yet state schooling in capitalist society has established a monopoly over educational production, and few would think of schooling their children anywhere else. It is in schools that children learn the language and culture of the nation and society. It is there they learn the existing social relations that will dominate their lives both in school and at work when they become adults. Schools are where the social relations of production are made legitimate. The production of educational knowledge has within it the ideological consequence of reaffirming the subordinate and inferior position of students. It condemns their language, thus condemning the class positions, language, and culture of their families.

Of course, these condemnations are not apparent on the surface of classroom life. The idea of free, universal, and equal education is an ideological construct that has strong support in most capitalist systems. It emphasizes the idea that individuals can go as far as they wish based on their abilities. This is one of the ways schools organize their work and evaluation methods. Althusser, Bourdieu, and others are correct when they see ideology as a problem that distorts what is really happening in classrooms and schools. But such ideologies have developed from the lived experiences of individuals. They are real for the people who experience them and often have a great deal of logical, empirical evidence to support them. An individual student, Maria could, as one mode of adoption, be ashamed of her family because they don't speak English and have to live in a poorer part of town. This shows that they haven't been able to earn much money and that her mother, who is the sole support of the family, is not an able or educated person. This is a reality that Maria lives with every day. It influences the neighborhood school she attends and the kind of experiences she has in her classrooms. Maria might feel ashamed of her mother, and of herself, too. She might not like the way she has to dress each day and the way others make fun of her foreign accent. Only later might she begin to understand her family's experiences in a different way. She might come to see how guilty her mother felt when she could not raise her family in a safer, more secure neighborhood. She might realize that her mother had been taught to see herself in a very negative way, too, and that she had passed some of these feelings on to her.

Maria has been taught to believe that a person's social status in society reflects her ability to do difficult intellectual work. This has been a reality for her and for her family. They have not been able to get better jobs because they do not have the educational credentials to qualify for them. This has made her feel that she comes from an inferior family, a lesser social and ethnic group. It has left her confused and deeply troubled about her feelings toward her mother, brothers, and sisters. Maria doesn't like to visit them now that she is older. But somewhere she knows that her schooling taught her to be ashamed of her own poverty and her cultural and linguistic heritage. She was taught to accept the inequalities in society because they were based on educational merit and achievement.

It is necessary to return to Althusser to show that, for him, the production of theoretical knowledge is something that should not be grounded in human experience.[8] With this, we disagree. Such deterministic theories cannot help people like Maria to struggle with the conditions of their existence. Certainly the Althusserian insights into the importance of the methods and structure of communications is worthy of study and can deepen our understanding of educational production in modern society. But, as we shall show in chapter 4, theories that deny totally the subjectivity and consciousness of the individual cannot be helpful in the struggle to unravel the web of affiliations involved in the construction of the individual in modern society.

Althusser dissolves the personal experiences of individuals into misrecognized and misunderstood irrelevancies. In his hands, they become not individual experiences but common social and political events. He questions the reality of individual experiences and places ideology above them as more real and constant. Others, like Gramsci, have shown how individual experiences can be both personal and sociohistorical. Althusser, however, doesn't allow for possibilities outside of his rationalized system. Following the work of structural Marxists, Althusser postulates that individuals are merely automatic outcomes of capitalist modes of production. In his work, the social and historical events that led up to present conditions seem irrelevant. So are the contradictions we experience every day in our work and schooling. In the world of the de-centered individual, one cannot alter one's behavior or increase one's understanding of political or economic practice. It is only within a new way of producing wealth or knowledge that individuals could find any hope of living and working with others in more humane ways.

Young people in high school, weary from boredom, regimentation, and continual test-taking, might be led to think about why their schoolwork is so irrelevant, so undemocratic in its presentations and classroom structures. They might begin to wonder how much they are really learning and whether schools are the best place to learn. They might think about how living and working with others in a more cooperative way might improve their present conditions. They might also think about how much they are learning about themselves and the way that teachers teach in their crowded, impersonal classrooms. They might even begin to ask questions that they have not allowed to come to consciousness: What do I want to read, what do I want to learn in these schools? Have I bothered to understand what is being taught to me? They might wonder why understanding things is less important than doing what one is told, than preparing for the tests that seem so important to teachers and parents. These examples show that individuals don't live in ahistorical, immutable worlds. Their sense of themselves and their society, no matter how distorted by linguistic categories and ideologies, is lived out by attention to needs and wants, in a desire to change situations and learn more about themselves. Ideological production does a good job of obscuring the real condition of life for most individuals, but they can break out of this condition. Much of their identity is ideologically and linguistically defined, but, as we will show, individuals can come to learn more about themselves, even if they do this with the imperfect tools of language and ideology. They can become subjects, even though they most often appear to be objects manipulated by forces they cannot see, hear, or comprehend. They can develop knowledge, which can be sufficient for effecting changes in the social relations of schooling and society.

Such a break in symbolic controls involves discourse, as Bernstein has shown.[9] Discourse at home and in schools transforms the consciousness of individuals, helping dominated and dominant groups to recognize one another. It also facilitates the maintenance of power and control by the dominant classes in society, bringing cultural and linguistic codes into everyday social intercourse.

Bernstein, following Bourdieu, believes that a field of symbolic control exists and that such control is the responsibility of a set of agencies that specialize in ideological transmissions. These agencies are akin to the ideological state apparatuses Althusser and Gramsci identified in their analyses of the reproduction processes in modern society. Youngsters learn the proper ways to relate to the world of work, school, and society. How should they think and feel about what is happening to them as women, minorities, or members of the poorer classes? What forms of consciousness should they develop to shield them from the prejudices and insults they will face in their interactions with dominant others? What can they expect once they enter the world of schooling or work? Most important of all, what kind of attitudes should they develop in order to function best in a confusing and confused world? In chapter 5, we speak of the exploitation that emanates from the social relations of production in the workplace. The capitalists regulation of the means of production and the conditions under which labor can be employed establishes their control in a very real and tangible manner. The attitudes and demeanor of management and owners are quite different from those of workers, which are coded in ways easily understood by both groups. But under symbolic control, the dominance takes more muted, discursive forms. In the workplace, the interdependence between employees and capital is explicit and observable, even as we admit that such relations carry with them dominance and domination of one class over another. In symbolic control, the families, schools, and so on seem unrelated to the economic sector. Their ideological effects are hidden beneath their specialized activities of socialization and education.

Bernstein distinguished between the differing agencies involved in symbolic control and the codes they used to transmit their ideologies. Agents were identified as scientists, doctors, architects, psychologists, and administrators, as well as families and schools, which specialize in the symbolic control of youth. Other agencies, such as theaters, art galleries, films, television, publishers, and newspapers, are in the economic sector of society, but they use ideology to control communications that influence the identity and world views of individual citizens. These latter agencies are different from those agencies which function only in the symbolic control arena because of their social organization and the profit-and-loss functions they must observe. They offer services or products, performing their work in clinics, small businesses, or as professionals hiring themselves out to interested clients. Other agents of symbolic control write texts for state schools, newspapers and magazines, actors, and editors and others who work with language and symbols. These people may create the texts, but they do not have power over their use or dissemination. They do not have the know-how or power to market these creations. Agencies that produce such products must deal with conflicting values: they must show a profit, even as they seek to market socially redeeming texts or productions.

For Bernstein, the ideological orientations of individuals are a consequence of their class position in the social and occupational hierarchy.[10] People who work in schools, hospitals, business offices, and research laboratories are apt to have different interests and concerns, different identities. Yet their common identity as professionals may be much less important than their location and position in the hierarchy of symbolic control agencies.

Bernstein indicates that there may be conflict between persons working in the fields of symbolic control and those in the economic sectors of society. The latter may be more interested in public expenditures for their particular bureaucratic agencies; the former may have an interest in restricting the state's expenditures and influence. Thus the role of the state can be an arena of conflict between these two groups.

Following these ideas, Bernstein defined three agents of education and production: The ruling class, or those who have decisive power to decide the methods, contexts, and usage of physical resources; those who control the means, contexts, and possibilities of cultural communications and transmissions in agencies that deal with problems of symbolic control; and the working classes, who are ultimately dominated by production practices and symbolic control discourses and institutions.

THE WOMEN'S MOVEMENT: POWER AND DOMINANCE IN THE CAPITALIST ORDER

Certain groups have forced themselves into the consciousness of society during the past decades. Women began to raise again serious issues of equity and fairness in the 1960s and 1970s. They became concerned with human needs and identity problems in a society that seemed to have forgotten their importance. They questioned the traditional view that well-being meant only possessing material attributes of shelter, clothing, and an ability to consume factory-produced commodities. Even though many wanted nothing more than a place in the capitalist order, they were forced to confront the realities of power and dominance as these were played out in their homes and workplaces. The women's liberation movement, or the movement to proletarianize women as some prefer to call it, forced millions of women out of their homes and into the labor force. Some did so willingly, seeking positions in middle and upper management or greater financial independence. But many more had to take menial positions, as they had done for centuries, work that paid them poorly. Working influenced women's feelings about themselves and those with whom they worked. Their sense of worth and their individual identities changed, and they had to struggle with problems of dual loyalty to their families and to the firms that employed them. They began to think about themselves and their social conditions in new ways, thinking more about their own needs and concerns, their careers, and their abilities to compete with men who earned more for doing similar kinds of work. Many became aware of how their class position determined their daily work and home experiences. Their aspirations were tempered by these insights and by how women were treated in the workplace and in society. Others, ignoring the worker-capital focus of classical Marxism, with its asexual worker, began to focus on what their experiences were telling them: there was a conflict between men and women that often affected the ways in which women lived and worked. The women's movement tried to break through the ideologies, stereotypes, and hidden messages of the workplace. It taught that the two sexes were different and had to be talked about in terms of these differences.

It is the women's movement that has struggled with the problems associated with working mothers and their children. It is these women who have wondered about the naturalness of domesticity and the nature of such responsibilities. Some few of them have learned that subordination of women in the workplace serves the function and purposes of capital, which is always looking for cheap, dependable labor. They have begun to question their relationships with men and their history, which has not allowed them to see themselves as independent, self-reliant individuals. Many women are beginning to feel the need to challenge the ideology of subordination, which has deep roots in our culture's past. They are forcing men to think about the ways in which they see women, and they are changing the mores and moral understandings that govern sexual relations. More and more, middle-class women are challenging their subordination. They have learned that they cannot improve their social condition without ending their inferior and secondary status vis-à-vis men; they can no longer find the meaning of their own lives by subordinating themselves to the needs of their husbands and children. Of course these insights apply less to working-class and minority women, who have had different experiences in the workplace.

Women, in trying to break out of the stereotypical and ideological constructs of traditional society, have profound problems. The ways in which women are taught to keep their place, to be subservient and obedient to men and to their filial responsibilities, are profound and learned in the family and schools. The attempt to fight this socialization has been met with self-doubt among some women and with distaste by others who have accepted the old ways of thinking about their situation. Yet, the new thinking has challenged old ideas about what is and is not manly, which has been an opening that has altered the ways in which the sexes relate to one another. The structure and ways of doing things in families and at work are undergoing changes as women get a sense of their power to transform the social and economic conditions of their lives. This is true even as we are forced to admit that many women in the working classes have not benefited much from any of these changes. Millions are still living in poverty, with little chance to realize themselves or to make a reasonably secure life for their children. Althusser, on the other hand, would not give these experiences much importance.[11] He sees women as being defined and identified by the linguistic and cultural categories of capitalist production. He gives no attention or value to the contradictions that appear and reappear in the lives of women, in their efforts to redefine their own perceptions about the sexes. But without some ability to act as a subject, a doer, women are doomed to remain as they have been since the dawn of history. Therefore, we are forced to seek evidences that, despite the linguistic construction of much of the individual's identity, there are other elements which contribute to the individual's uniqueness and ability to struggle against the mimetic structures of the past.

Of course, Althusser's emphasis on ideology helps us to understand why it is so difficult to change people's perceptions and understandings. The institutions that women are seeking to change have endured and seem rooted in atavistic cultures of the distant past. Since ideology is a lived way of thinking, the work of women can be seen as fitting into that definition of the term. But by using Althusser's methods of reading texts, women and others who believe in more egalitarian ways of living together can analyze the messages they are given and begin to develop knowledge that helps them to move forward out of their subordinate, dependent statuses. Althusser has shown that he understands why it is necessary for women to remain subordinate in capitalist production, but he does not seem to believe that a group that has only recently achieved citizenship and political power can successfully challenge the power of the dominant classes and ideologies in society. He also appears to believe that gaining knowledge of an ideology does not necessarily signal the beginning of the end of that ideology. For, in knowing what an ideology is, what its knowledge and structure is, what its logic and reason for being is, comes also, paradoxically, a knowledge of why it was needed and necessary in the first place.

A RESTATEMENT

We may summarize by referring again to sociocultural theories of schooling as perspectives that study the relations between educational systems and capitalism. Educational production comes to be seen as an essential activity of the state, reproducing the labor power and citizenry of the nation.

Sociocultural theories of schooling are also concerned with the ideological effects that suffuse this form of production. Ideology provides individuals with explanations and rationalizations about themselves and their relations to others. It is based on facts in their everyday lives. Ideology uses language and thoughts to provide individuals with ideas about themselves, ideas they learn in their infancy. Ideologies are a natural outgrowth of social systems and represent the way people live and interpret interactions in their daily lives.

It becomes of immediate interest, then, that we understand what needs these ideologies fulfill. Perhaps the most important need is to think of the individual as a subject, capable of understanding and acting in his or her own interests. A second important need is to explain why we are living and how we should live as citizens and workers.

So far as ideology is concerned, its primary purpose is to bind people to one another. It is a form of social cement that brings people together in social structures and agencies. It provides teachers and students with rationales for their behaviors in classrooms. In the process of educational production, teachers and students use language or signification codes to communicate. The messages allow them to get through the school day, but they do not allow them to think about what is happening to them. That comes later, when teachers and students reflect on what has transpired. They attempt to transform the past into language, thus distorting it and inducing ideological effects. Most of the time they confuse their linguistic constructions with the realities they experienced in classrooms, unaware of the ways words and ideas transform events.

Structural Marxists have developed a tradition that sees the individual as an object who cannot escape his ideological understanding of himself or his world. This is because linguistic and cultural distortions make it impossible for him to act. Individuals are not seen as real subjects but as make-believe ones who exist only in the stream of consciousness and linguistic categories of others.

Here, the importance of the family appears. It is in the family that the neonate moves from nature to civilization, from animalistic needs to language and an understanding of himself as a human being in a social world. When students take this personal identity into the classrooms, a conflict occurs. Schooling forces youngsters to reevaluate themselves according to their abilities to master the language and culture of the educational system. This reevaluation provides students with an institutional identity, one which places them as a male or a female, a black or a white person, and so on.

Because schooling is an instrument of political structures, its goals are necessarily related to those of the state. Its curriculum, pedagogies, and evaluation methods attempt to fulfill schooling's mandate: the reproduction of the labor force in capitalist production.

The problems of human consciousness are always framed in the ideological understandings of a particular historical period. The intent of structural Marxists can best be understood by reviewing the historical era in which they were framed. This is done in chapter 3, when we discuss post-WW II Europe and the collapse of the French colonial empire. A century of global warfare, economic depression, and social revolutions seemed to lend themselves to the idea that persons cannot act consciously in their own interests. These ideas are contested by the writer, who cites the activities of the woman's movement as an example of conscious actions to change ideological perceptions about this subordinate group.

2

The Role of the State

When we ask the question, "How did modern educational systems originate?" we are also asking, "Why does the state fund, license, and operate such agencies?" Had it not been for the modern nation-state, universal compulsory education might never have occurred. A study of the state's role seems necessary if we are to gain a clearer insight into the nature and history of the schooling enterprise. For this, we begin by looking at the state as it was understood in the last century. Then we provide the reader with a short history of schooling in the United States, emphasizing the state as enforcer and intervener in the educational system. Finally we discuss recent theories that view the state as a structure internally related to other agencies and institutions in modern capitalist systems.

Anyone who reads Marx's ideas about the state will conclude they are incomplete, at best. Marx was concerned primarily with the evolution of capitalism in the mid–nineteenth century. Perhaps his earliest views of the state are set forth in the *Critique of the Hegelian Philosophy of Right*.[1] In this work, the state is seen as a guardian of the general interest of civilization, society, and law, echoing Hegel's thoughts. It is the social institution within which moral, political, educational, and judicial freedoms reside. The individual, in submitting himself to the state, acts in accordance with his own interest and nature, his own reason.

But as his work matured, Marx paid greater attention to the ways in which the state was influenced and driven by external pressures.[2] Already he saw Hegel's views on the state as too abstract; they dehumanized the state, setting it apart from the people who had created it. Hegel correctly acknowledged the separation and conflict that existed between the state and civil society, yet he believed that these were somehow fused or reconciled in the state itself. The contradictions between the state and society were resolved artificially in Hegel's thought. The alienation of the individual from the power of the state, the conflict between the individual as a private citizen following one's own interests and concerns while also a citizen of the state, was resolved by an idealized version of the state's goals and functioning in society.

Marx believed that these ideas were an attempt to mystify, not to explain the contradiction between the state and society. Conflict or political alienation was the core of political struggle. Man's political significance was detached from his real, private circumstances. Yet this condition determined social identity and class. The mediating features of the state described by Hegel were supposed to resolve the contradictions between the individual's interests and those of the state through the use of bureaucracy, rulers, the middle classes, the legislatures, and so on. But Marx believed they were incapable of doing this. Private interests would make themselves felt, to the detriment of the interests of the majority. Writing in the middle and latter part of the nineteenth century, Marx asked a key question: "What power does the state have over private property?" The state gave the illusion of controlling private property, yet it was property that paid for and controlled those who administered the state. The state subdued the individual and social wills of the collectivity only to turn these over to the will of private property. This became the state's real reason for being, its moral, political basis for existence. Private interests also controlled the schools by owning the government that funded, licensed, and operated them. This was detrimental to the poor, the minorities, and women, who had little or no power over private property and the instruments of production. Schools gave the illusion of interest in the welfare of students, yet the socioeconomic condition of a student's family was the single most important factor in determining success or failure in schools.

In these early writings, Marx still thought of conflict between the state and society as a political problem. Ideas of democracy and constitutional government were admired as ideal solutions to the political alienation of society from its state structures. Of course, Marx was writing at a time when democracy and monarchy were still struggling with one another. Property was the same in all states, but this insight was not yet a part of Marx's analysis. But he had, in his *Critique*, already come to the idea that political liberty or emancipation would not necessarily lead to the emancipation of the human race. In other works, he pointed to the fact that the state could free itself from certain constraints, without affecting the individuals who lived in that state. Nevertheless, Marx saw political advancement as a monumental achievement in the history of human development even as he cautioned that it was not its final form. Rather it was the last form of human freedom before the old existing social order collapsed. The freeing of the individual could only be accomplished by passing beyond bourgeois society. Preceding Tonnies, Marx saw that mercantile society was destroying the gemeinschaft and replacing it with use relationships grounded in greed, avariciousness, competitiveness, and the isolation of the individual. Trade, money, and the commercial spirit were alienating persons from their work and from social relationships, which had always given human existence meaning in the past. Only a new society that humanized and rationalized the needs of individuals could provide an environment in which alienation could be reversed.

Writing in 1843 and 1844, Marx now believed that man had the need and the right to overthrow all political conditions that enslaved him, making him an abandoned and contemptible object. For the first time he spoke of the proletariat as the force that could lead to an end to the old social order. Marx was, during this period, a supporter of the political emancipation movements developing throughout Europe. These tended to make the state more accessible to a larger number of individuals. The state that was representative and democratic was the ultimate achievement of the bourgeois system, ending the exclusive privileges of the aristocratic system and the encumbrances and constraints of the past. But again, political emancipation was seen as an incomplete victory that could be undermined by private property's ability to buy and sell politicians and other agencies of the state.

In the *German Ideology*, Marx and Engels went into more detail about the relationship between bourgeois society and the state.[3] They concluded that laws were always an expression of the economic relations that prevailed at the time. These ideas were expressed more clearly in *The Communist Manifesto*, in which the state was seen as nothing more than an instrument for one class to oppress another.

Writing about the most advanced countries in Europe, Marx modified his views. The ruling class, as a collectivity, did not control the state. Rather it was only a small part of that class that, at one time or another, had such control and dominance. Those who actually operated the state might belong to other, less dominant classes. This would not affect the state's role as the defender of the interests of property, but it would introduce more complicated forms of cooption and adaption of other classes to the laws that state agencies passed.

Of course Marx was fully aware of dictatorial rule of the state, such Bonapartism, which controlled France during much of this period.[4] One-man rule was a triumph over the parliament and the legislative power in France. It was a victory for the executive power over parliament. The nation, acting through the dictator or emperor, made the will of the dominant, ruling classes the will of the nation. Everything was given over to the executive power of the emperor, to his will, his authority. France was now under the control of the individual, but this individual was supported by a military establishment that brought all classes to their knees. Marx spoke of the enormous power executive leaders possessed. In their hands were concentrated large bureaucracies, military, and police forces, functionaries who were appointed by and owed their positions to the leader. These were the means through which the bourgeoisie now ruled in France. Referring to the triumph of the second Bonaparte, Marx observed that the state appeared to be an independent, separate entity, with Louis Napoleon as its head.

These comments seemed to place Marx in a position where he viewed the state as separate and apart from the interests of any class. But he was quick to add, "And the state power is not suspended in mid-air. Bonaparte represents a class, and the most numerous class of French society at that, the small-holding peasants." Yet these peasants were disorganized and lacked the cohesion they needed to rule effectively. This meant that Bonaparte was needed as their representative, master, and authority. To follow their interests, they had to agree to the unlimited governmental power that protected them from other classes.

Of course Louis Napoleon believed that his mission was to save France for the bourgeoisie and the middle classes. To do this, he was obliged to break their political power and the power of others who might not like their place in the new order. Marx noted the contradictory nature of the man and his governmental tasks and the political acts that humiliated first one class and then another to keep them off balance and weak. Finally, Marx showed that Bonapartism was not neutral among the contending classes. It was not instituted for the benefit of the entire society, as it liked to pretend. Its reason for being was to maintain the old social order and the control and domination of capital over the new forms of labor that had evolved with the industrial movement.

Writing many years later, after Marx's death, Engels noted that there were periods in which the exception did occur. Warring classes balanced one another, and the power of the state seemed to acquire a certain independence from all factions. But this idea of the state's independence seemed to go further than anything which Marx had considered. For Marx, in the last analysis, Bonapartism was the protector of the economically and socially dominant classes.

In the *Critique of Hegel's Philosophy*, Marx showed how the state bureaucracy sought to change the state's purposes into the purposes of the bureaucracy, to make them one and the same thing. And in Grundisse he spoke of the despotic states that held themselves above all lesser classes and communities. The state was seen as the dominant force in Asian societies, and those who administered it were society's real rulers.

Marx differentiated between the democratic and representative republic and the dictatorship of the proletariat. They had little, if anything, in common. Marx had denounced the class character of the democratic republic, seeing it as, in reality, a plutocracy. Nevertheless, he supported its coming into being in his lifetime as an advance over what had been in the past. Democratic and representative republics were the most advanced type of government for bourgeois society, and a decided improvement over the feudal systems. But they maintained class rule, the rule of the bourgeoisie, which meant that the masses of humanity were still dominated. The limitations of the democratic republic were made clear in the *Address of the Central Committee of the Communist League*, which he wrote with Engels in 1850. The democratic, petty bourgeois state strives for changed social conditions in order to benefit from these new conditions. Such conditions will allow it to diminish and control the state expenditures and bureaucracies, to shift the main burden of taxes onto other segments of society, to establish public agencies of credit, and to create bourgeois property relations in the countryside, replacing those of the feudal period. To do all this, they will need allies, and especially the support of the peasant majorities. For workers, however, they wish only better wages and a more secure environment. In this way they hope to wean workers from their revolutionary attitudes.

Poulantzas, writing a century later, define the state as an intervening agency at every level of society, attempting to produce cohesion and social solidarity among the different classes.[5] This is done to maintain the predominant mode of production and the continued control and domination of the possessing classes. Capitalism's essence is its ability to develop economic surpluses from the exchange relations that develop once production has been completed. The state insures that the conditions for these economic exchanges are maintained and strengthened. This is essentially a structural analysis of the political and judicial systems in capitalist societies, ignoring historical perspectives. The practices of the state go beyond the mere pursuit of the dominant classes' interests and concerns, however. They include unifying the social system and establishing ententes between the different power blocs and classes. The rulers or administrators of the state may not be from the ruling classes themselves, as the Richard Nixon presidency illustrated in the late 1960s and early 1970s. Yet this unifying function of the state, especially in its legal, national, and ideological aspects, allows individuals to see themselves as isolated subjects who are governed by juridical systems. Class memberships are blurred, and the unity of such formations rendered irrelevant and useless.

Domination in capitalist systems is possible because states appear as national entities, not completely dominated by the economic interests of the dominant classes or factions. They appear to be timeless givens, mimetic structures that individuals have to deal with when they enter into social relations in society. This is accomplished by ideological and political unity among the people of all classes, which allows the state to secure support and consent of the weaker, dominated classes. Through the use of ideological state apparatuses and the coercion of law, representative democracies become advanced forms of the capitalist political state. In order to achieve national consensus in such states, compromises are necessary on every level of decision- and policy-making. The dominated classes are permitted their own ideological institutions, such as unions, political parties that pursue their interests and exact concessions, and common schools. However, these are always granted within the prevailing system of economic domination of possessing classes over weaker ones. Capitalist democracy does not provide a means by which the fundamental system of class domination can be changed.

Finally, some brief remarks should be made about the effects of this interventionist character of the capitalist state in the establishment and maintenance of educational systems. One important role of the state is to reproduce the social and economic conditions of production and the work force, generation after generation. It is in its need to safeguard and insure the conditions within which trade, commerce, and production occur that the history and nature of schooling can be grasped. It is in their need to provide youth with moral suasion that the authoritarian social structure and physical size of educational institutions can best be understood. Since its inception in the precapitalist period, schooling has been involved with problems of religion, politics, poverty, and urban conflict. During the Reformation in Europe, it was based on the idea that reading the Bible was an important path to salvation. Luther strongly supported the belief that education should be made available to all; that the state should make available and constrain its citizens to partake of it.[6] The Lutheran and Calvinist traditions both had as their cardinal belief that all needed an education that would permit them to read the Scriptures. In the 1600s, compulsory education was mandated in the Duchies of Weimar and Gotha. In Holland, the Synod of Dort tried to establish compulsory education in its schools, and in 1646 the Scotch Parliament ordered the establishment of compulsory schooling for its youth.

An entire network of state-mandated education took hold in the German provinces. King Frederick William I undertook in 1717, to provide such education for all of his citizens, saying they would be obliged by law to send their children to school daily in the winter and at least twice a week in the summer. Financing for such schools was to be provided by community funds. By 1794 these laws had been codified so that instruction in school had to continue until the child was found to have the knowledge needed to function as a rational adult. Even at this early period in the history of schooling, a certain significance was attached to the socializing powers of education: that which had been thrust upon the stage of history as a religious requirement of conscience was now used by state authorities to pacify and unite citizens. In little more than a century, state-supported education had become the norm for many of the emerging bourgeois states of central and northern Europe.

A SHORT HISTORY OF SCHOOLING IN THE UNITED STATES

In 1642 the Massachusetts General Court ordered selectmen to observe if parents and apprentice masters were preparing their children "to read and understand the principles of religion and the capital laws of the country."[7] They further sought to learn whether youngsters were being trained "in learning and labor." This was the first instance of a legislative body in the English-speaking world ordering that all children be taught to read. In 1647 the Massachusetts Court ordered the establishment of schools so that compulsory attendance could be more easily enforced, providing the foundations upon which the state-supported common schools movement created itself a century later. Still, compulsory education never took hold in the Anglican colonies of the New World and in England. The act of compulsion conferred upon schooling a governmental and social sanction that provided a haven for institutional development and learning. It organized the social world into a coherent unity that ethically judged and evaluated the worth and competency of students and teachers alike. Perhaps it was repulsion felt toward the confinement and loss of liberty that such education demanded that caused the colonies and later the United States not to pursue state schools and compulsory education during the seventeenth and eighteenth centuries. France did not embrace state-supported compulsory education until 1882; England did not provide comprehensive laws until the twentieth century.

Compulsory education was a legal response to the social problems of poverty, urbanism, and industrialism as they were first being experienced in the nineteenth century. Legal, in the precise sense that the emerging legal-rational era gave to it—the structuring of learning by the state so that citizens could be more easily fitted into the new machine culture. The authority of schools was derived from the state, and its function was to transform youth into productive workers and citizens. The school was accepted by society because it congregated children in a professional setting and rendered them obedient and harmless. Schools were like a well-disciplined workplace, a military encampment, a detention center; yet the intent and the intensity were obviously different. The educational system's authority was based on the legal mandates of the state and the ideology and common understandings of the people. These made the schools seem like natural places for civilizing the savage nature of youth; it gave schools the responsibility for reproducing the economic and social conditions and belief systems of society.[8]

From the beginning, schooling was concerned with depriving youth of idle, free time, curing them of their vagrant and criminal tendencies. Schooling was not merely a place to learn the rudiments of reading, writing, and arithmetic. It was also a preparation of youth for their future in industrial society.[9] It was an initiation into the behaviors and norms of the workplace. Schools had similar relationships and authority structures, even though they were based on legal-rational structures that ended with the school day. Youngsters were taught to obey no matter what they were told to do. Their bodies were controlled by teachers who expected them to remain seated and attentive throughout the school day. Without permission, they were not permitted to leave the room. They had to prove their right to be present in other parts of the building whenever they were confronted by teachers. They were ordered to compete even when their chances for success were limited or nonexistent. Different types of schools were established to provide tracks for youngsters from different social classes, thus constraining and delimiting the occupational possibilities of such youngsters in their adult lives. Still the value of education as a path to economic opportunity and success persisted in ideological thought:

> Is anyone willing to give an ignorant farm laborer as much as he is ready to pay for the services of an intelligent man? And if not, why the distinction? And if an ignorant man is not the best man upon a farm, is he likely to be so in the shop or mill? . . . All classes of employers are equally concerned in the education of the laborer, for learning not only makes his labor more valuable to himself, but the market price of the product is generally reduced, and the change affects favorably all interests of society.[10]

Let us return for a moment to the first compulsory attendance proposals and the Massachusetts state edict of 1852, which led to attendance laws in most states of the Union by the end of the century. From the first, state laws set themselves the task of ameliorating the social disorganization and dislocation that accompanied urban growth, poverty, and massive immigration. Although these laws were largely unenforced during most of the century, they were used to reduce urban delinquency in some northeastern states. Crime and increasing pockets of urban slums worsened in this period. The number of poor and immigrant families multiplied rapidly, as it was to do for the rest of the century. But it was not until 1849 that an alarming increase in the rate of crime caused the Boston School Committee to propose compulsory education for all its children. It was decided that those Irish children who did not work in factories or attend schools were outside the control and purview of the state and society; a law subjecting them to arrest and incarceration in reform schools was strongly urged. Youngsters would be sent to such prison schools for larceny, vagrancy, stubbornness, truancy, and so on. But soon the number of truants in these children's prisons became ruinous, with Irish immigrant boys disproportionately represented: the Boston marshal began to compile statistics on the numbers of truant and vagrant boys in such reform schools; it was shown that most were from impoverished and foreign parentage.[11]

This was the era of Horace Mann's writings on the value of educated labor in 1842, of George S. Boutwell's writing on educated labor and industrialization in 1859. During this period, the labor force in the United States was revolutionized by the appearance of new forms of machine technology and communication. As the size of business enterprises increased, the need for literate, educated labor also increased. It was this need and the increasing population of immigrant and urban poor that prompted the Board of Public Charities of the State of Pennsylvania to propose compulsory education laws in 1871: A state with so many neglected children, a youth population rendered unemployable by ignorance and idle habits, was a danger to the social peace and tranquility of society. The proposal proclaimed the duty of the state to look after and educate those unfortunate children who had nowhere else to turn.[12]

In this struggle to gather in and school the youth, the enactment of compulsory education laws was certainly a victory for those who wished to establish common schools, for those who believed that states had a duty to prepare youth for adulthood and their places in the labor market. Voluntary attendance was supplanted by legal coercion and the threat of confinement in reform schools or houses of correction; the culturally and linguistically disabled were not to be excluded from attendance in common state schools; youngsters who had little aptitude for book learning were no longer excused. They were accepted into the classroom, in the belief that every child could benefit from ordinary classroom routines and discipline. A mutual system of responsibility and duty was established between the state and the children who resided in them. Youth had a right and a duty to attend schools, to receive training. States had an obligation to intercede, providing state schools that could train children in the types of behaviors and attitudes they would need to succeed in their adult lives.

THE SILENT POOR

Immigration to the United States fell into two distinct periods. Initially, the first settlers were English, with the exception of a small Dutch settlement at New Amsterdam and a colony of Swedish Lutherans in the area now known as the state of Delaware. The dominance of English names in the census of 1790 bears this out. Only a handful of non–English speaking colonies were in existence at this time.[13]

As a matter of record, immigration before 1820 consisted mostly of white, Anglo-Saxon, and Protestant people; the distinguishing characteristic of new arrivals before 1840 was most often their indigent status. In 1842, 100,000 immigrants entered the United States. Thereafter, immigration never fell below this figure in any one year for the remainder of the century. In the decade from 1847 to 1857 to the number of newcomers was never less than 200,000, and in 1854 it reached 420,833 persons. From 1820 to 1840, a migration of German and Irish peoples occurred, creating a crisis over Catholic parochial schools in Massachusetts. This was the beginning of the second phase of the immigration experience, because the Irish were considered to be of different and inferior racial stock. The Germans, on the other hand, proved to be more acceptable. They were thought to be not much different in origin from the first English settlers themselves: courageous, intelligent, resourceful, adaptable, and self-reliant individuals. The situation reached critical dimensions after 1882, when the character and background of the immigrant changed significantly. Armies of silent poor immigrated from Southern and Eastern Europe: By 1890, 20,000 Italians were arriving each year; and from 1906 to 1910 as many as 1,180,000 reached our shores. In the decade between 1903 and 1914, immigration added 750,000 to 1,250,000 newcomers. After 1880, a host of nationalities from Austria, Poland, and the Balkans, Jews from Russia, and Japanese and Koreans from Asia swelled the tide of immigration. Many more came from other parts of Europe and Canada.

The Southern and Eastern Europeans were thought to be racially different and inherently inferior to the native population. They were seen as illiterate, passive persons with little self-initiative. They had little or no conception of Anglo-Saxon culture with its ideas of liberty, law, government, and public decency. They weakened and corrupted the political processes of the republic. These new arrivals settled in northern cities and in the middle and far West, creating a serious problem in "housing and living, moral and sanitary conditions" and the like because of their slovenly habits and life-styles. State schools found it difficult to adjust to these newcomers because, most often, they did not even speak the English language. Foreign mannerisms, customs, and language became dominant in some urban communities; and the schools were given the formidable task of transforming and Americanizing this foreign rabble. By 1910, the census showed 10,000,000 and more foreign-born persons living and working in the United States. Many could not read or write, and their patriotism was openly questioned by native Americans, who appreciated their value as cheap labor but who hated their alien ways. The immigrants tended to huddle together in ghettos where they could speak their native languages and enjoy familiar customs. Even their children were sometimes sent to non–English speaking parochial schools to maintain their cultural heritage.

State schools were given the job of assimilating these aliens into American life. They were asked to provide them with a common English language, an understanding of common law and government, freedom, free schools, and a tolerance for others and the prevailing economic system. These goals were in addition to the already-stated ones of socializing and transforming urban youth into compliant and productive workers. Now it was their additional task to mitigate the separating tendencies of alien languages and cultures by providing immigrant children with a common schooling that Americanized them and gave them greater access to the labor market.

The urban and immigrant poor were crowded into classrooms of immense size with children who often were much younger than they were.[14] They were forced into seats meant for eight-year-olds until they could learn to read and work in English. Then they were sent to other congested classrooms that were on their grade level, classrooms that often had sixty and more students in them.

The idea of immigrant children as aliens and animals, dangerous to themselves and society, was widely held. Education took its practices from the past and from its pressing need to establish order and control in crowded schools. Those students who were forced to sit in silence and obey without question were described as "wretched refuse" by the inscription that welcomed them on the Statue of Liberty. State schooling, at this point in time, was asked to make loyal "Americans, productive workers, and affluent citizens out of . . . human garbage."[15] This view of the immigrant youth as alien, unworthy, and incompetent prevailed in urban schools and gave them their somber atmosphere, their look of penal servitude. Education was less than ever linked to learning alone. At its center were the correction and reformation of the immigrant child's language, culture, moral outlook, and inner self. The alien nature of such youth could be transformed only by severe discipline and a rejection of their parental heritage and values. The theme of the Americanization of the immigrants was effectively projected during this period, in an attempt to gain support from the newcomers themselves. State schooling was held in high esteem by many immigrant families, and adults often attended night school to learn English and become citizens.

A punitive discipline and pedagogy, which had been inherited from the Lancastrian schools of the early nineteenth century, was formalized and practiced in state schools. Still, education had an ever-increasing value for immigrants. That value was linked to their desire to become full-fledged Americans and to learn the ways of their adopted country. But those hopes were seldom fully realized. State schooling did not prove to be a panacea for the social and economic dislocations of industrial capitalism. The discipline of the schools produced a barely literate citizenry, and dropout rates were very high. Immigrant youth were constantly made aware of just how unacceptable they were in their new country and how far they had to go before they could hope to do well in the competitive labor market. For newcomers, the value of schooling lay in the teaching of English and the opportunities such knowledge opened up for them in the job markets of industrialized America. For them, the socialization in state schools was an obvious rejection of their past heritages, which they often shared with school authorities! What was most painful, however, was the gulf that schooling created between the young and their immigrant parents. The ultimate goal was Americanization and the substitution of English for native European languages and culture. All efforts were focused on these goals of transformation, and the history, worth, and personal identities of immigrants and their children were devalued or ignored.

All these cultural and linguistic rejections of immigrants and their children, these practices woven into the very fabric of state schooling, had their effect. Silence, uniformity, and obedience were sanctified, reducing youth to a mechanical, authoritarian educational experience which prepared them only for their experiences on the job later in life. In state schools, education embraced the organizational structures and forms of punitive institutions. Students were separated and enclosed in classrooms that were the domain of teachers. They were forced to sit in silence and to move or speak only when asked to do so. In its uniformity and harshness, state schools acted as a legitimate monopoly in industrial society. They were the exclusive agency of the state charged with intervening to acculturate and prepare these alien youth for their places in the social and economic pyramid.

SCHOOLS FOR FAILURE

State schools at the turn of the century were criticized by only a few, perhaps because these institutions were shrouded in ideology and myth. Perhaps observers were unable to see the rejection and failure that accompanied the state pedagogy of forced acculturation and transformation.

One thing seemed undeniable: State schools were not educating immigrant and poor children effectively. They forced more and more of them to attend for longer and longer periods of time, yet the rate of their self-confessed failures was astounding. In Chicago in 1898, the schools reported that only 60 percent of the students attending school were at "normal age" grade level. The means and materials of education seemed to be in place in Chicago. The buildings, classrooms, teachers, and supplies were available. Yet the numbers of failing children were unacceptably high.[16] The numbers of those who were no longer in school, the number of dropouts, was not reported in this or other studies because they were no longer in attendance.

There were many reasons for this soaring failure rate. Those youngsters who dropped out of school had little chance to resume their studies later in life. Meanwhile, students who stayed in school were forced to experience a schooling that exposed them to constant rejection and failure. Of those who remained in the state schools, 40 percent were listed as below "normal age," whether they attended classes in Boston, Detroit, Philadelphia, Pittsburgh, New York, or Minneapolis. In Pittsburgh, 51 percent of the students were below "normal age" grade level; in Minneapolis the number of children who were failing rose to 65 percent. Between 1898 and 1917, the schools continued to release yearly reports, showing that more children were failing in schools than were succeeding there. As usual, these reports spoke only of those failures who were still in school.

These reports caused educators and politicians to seek stronger compulsory attendance laws, seeking to change the school-leaving age from twelve to fourteen. Later they sought to change it to sixteen, even though the dropout rates made a mockery of such laws. Students were kept in state schools for longer periods so that they would not burden an already overcrowded labor market. The problems of schooling urban poor and immigrant youth shifted from a concern about high failure rates to the problem of getting youngsters off the streets and into classrooms. In 1919, ten thousand work permits were issued to youngsters in Chicago; in 1930, that city issued only 987. Instead of holding back slow learners, some state schools began to pass upward large numbers of children who had failed their elementary schoolwork. They were retained in secondary schools now because of the limited employment opportunities that accompanied the onset of massive unemployment during the Great Depression. As late as 1931, George Strayer was acknowledging that extremely high failure rates were "still characteristic" of the majority of state schools in the United States.

State schools could not fail to produce large numbers of dropouts and failures because of the education they imposed on students. Whether youngsters were compelled to memorize facts or perform endless tasks of drill and rote recitation, from which there was no appeal and no end, it was, in the last analysis, a process that focused not on the youth but on the curriculum that had been arbitrarily selected by state authorities. It was a state schooling that established an artificial, closed world where the youngster's previous identities and experiences were irrelevant. State schools were given the task of schooling youth and reproducing the social relations of schools and society. By imposing a military discipline, they produced armies of truants and delinquents. They were charged with teaching respect for the laws and customs of American society, but their methods caused youngsters to fall behind and leave school at an early age. Politicians and educational reformers continued to insist on compulsory attendance for longer periods of time, pushing the failure rates into the upper grades throughout the 1920s, 1930s, and 1940s. Chicago reported a 65 percent increase in the number of failures among the underprivileged in their secondary schools as late as 1931. At the elementary level, retardation was reported at 61 percent of the total student population of survivors; and 41 percent of all students entering the ninth grade were seriously behind, too. In tenth grade the figure was 32 percent, but the number of dropouts was high and remained uncounted. Feeblemindedness, overcrowding, and poor family backgrounds were given as reasons for these high rates of student failure. They were duplicated in Boston, New York, Philadelphia, Detroit, and Washington, D.C. Thirteen thousand students studied in schools that were on half-day sessions; 60 percent were inadequately housed in urban schools as late as 1925. The Great Depression of the 1930s further worsened these conditions, while the 1940s and 1950s were preoccupied with global warfare and its aftermath. The 1960s saw a mounting crisis in the inner city schools of the United States and a struggle to achieve racial equality. By the 1970s and 1980s, poor conditions and student achievement had reached all-time lows. Conditions have not improved. New York city reported that Afro-American students were failing at the rate of 75 percent as late as 1988. Hispanic youth were (and are) failing at a 40 percent rate in the schools of Texas and California in 1989. Who were the students who failed in these congested state schools? In the first two decades of the twentieth century they were children and grandchildren of immigrants and the urban poor. Later, newer immigrants from every part of the world were joined by Afro-Americans who had migrated northward into the industrial cities. Education for acculturation and the needs of industrial labor markets gave state schools two compelling reasons for expanding their services: Americanization and the preparation of youth for their places in the occupational structure of society.[17]

These reasons for schooling were supported by the census of 1900, which showed 1.25 million of New York City's 3.5 million inhabitants were foreigners. Of the state school enrollment, 85 percent was made up of foreign-born children. State politicians and educators agreed that the schools had to return to their fundamental principles if these newcomers were to be effectively assimilated and taught in public schools.

The pedagogical principles these reformers referred to were enunciated at the beginning of this century and have changed little. State schooling must have as its primary goal the Americanization of the foreign born and their integration into the capitalist labor force. Schools are to be the great equalizer of the conditions of men, the agencies where the language and culture of the United States are provided for all students. Yet the schools of this period were overcrowded and poorly staffed. Half-time and part-time classes and truancy were reported by schoolmen on a regular basis. Common practice placed students in grades according to their ages, achievement levels, and deportment and the stage of their moral and patriotic development. The disadvantaged condition of certain students made it necessary for schoolteachers to alter established curricula. The progress of immigrant and urban poor students who were severely retarded had to be taken into account when one wished to evaluate a school district's performance or effectiveness. Since a cardinal principle of the state system of schooling was the transformation of the student's language and culture and his preparation for work in industrial society, it was important that youngsters be kept in school as long as possible. A standard curriculum was applied to all students, with a view to training them to see the world through the eyes of their teachers. This curriculum included the history and workings of American government and the use and appreciation of the English language. The economic system was considered a given in these schools, immutable and seldom discussed. The reward for good conduct and proficiency was the diploma, a document that certified success in school and opened up employment opportunities to the individual. Drill was one of the fundamental methods used to transform students into compliant, useful workers and citizens. Drill and rote recitation of facts must be thought of as training in the usage of time and effort. It must prepare the student to heed the instructions of his superiors, to do routine, boring work with diligence and care. Every youngster was obliged to be punctual and to memorize and practice his lessons. No student was allowed to remain idle in the classroom. The principle of continuous activity and work was rigidly followed, mimicking workplaces in the adult society.

This education of the urban poor and immigrant youth was both a societal effort to stem the tide of crime and poverty and an attempt to socialize and mold children into the American economic system. Yet the schools served to remind students of their impoverished condition and parentage: "schoolrooms stank . . . they were ill lit and ill ventilated . . . and rat infested."[18] The educational training focused upon the students' presumed future status and role in adult society. The principle of student selection, or tracking, was in place early in the nineteenth century and remained the core of the state schooling experiences of children in the United States. Americanization always meant making others accept the language of the dominant white Protestant culture and the assumptions of capitalist modes of economic and educational production.

If a primary function of state schools was to correct and transform the children of the immigrants and poor, then failure was to be expected. The level of educational achievement from 1890 onward was one of dismal failure accompanied by requests for more funding and resources. The reforms that were instituted did not change the functioning of state schools nor their social and intellectual insularity.

But these problems can be posed as questions: Who was served by these state institutions that failed myriads of children for more than a century?

What was the usefulness of these crowded state institutions that were constantly criticized and reformed? How did they manage to create the very delinquency they sought to eliminate? How did they reproduce the enormous numbers of dropouts from one decade to the next—dropouts they apparently sought to discourage. How did they produce the unbelievable rates of academic failure they themselves reported to the public each year? After forcing out these urban youth, state schools stigmatized them by depriving them of the certification needed to work in the better-paying occupations. The high school diploma became an important piece of paper delimiting the possibilities of millions of young men and women. These practices seemed quite functional for a stratified labor market, with its constantly high numbers of unemployed workers.

We can see that state schools, with their elaborate punishment and regimentation practices, were intended to educate youngsters into their proper places; to distribute and accustom them to a life of lower expectations and accomplishments. It was not just that American society wished to render youth docile and law-abiding, but that it wished to prepare them for an acceptance of the conditions of work that existed in the workplace. State schooling would then appear as a legitimate and fair way of handling differences in opportunity and access to the better-paying jobs and life-styles. By providing fair competition over the formative years of a student's life, state schools gave an objective accounting of a student's achievement. It provided a rationale for excluding the less worthy and incompetent, for neutralizing feelings of envy, jealousy, anger, and anxiety among those who would be assigned to the lesser places in the labor market. Schooling did not simply note the inequities in student deportment and achievement; it documented those differences, providing a scientific explanation that made them seem more important than they really were. If later these methods were shown to be invalid, it was only because the middle classes no longer controlled the rage and anger of those parents and community leaders whose children were sorted out by the previous pedagogic practices.

THE INTERVENTIONIST CHARACTER OF THE STATE IN MODERN TIMES

Reformists' strategies of schooling confuse democratic ideologies with the practices of state governments and their schools. Both the state and its educational systems espouse universal political representation and individual freedom. But, in fact, they exclude the children of the immigrant and poor from any effective representation or power. This difference between the ideological effects of bourgeois states (and their schools) and the actual consequences of their structures have three important features: The supposed separation of economics from politics leads to an exclusion of those who cannot pay off the politicians through campaign contributions or other means. A specialized group of politicians push the working and poorer classes out of the participation processes, as a specialized group of educators do in the public schools. Workers have little or no say in who will run for office, and students have no power to effect what will happen to them in their classrooms. A second feature is the debilitation of working-class and student organizations as they come to be seen as weak and ineffective organizations. This, in turn, leads to even less representation and individual freedom at the very moment that bourgeois legalisms are assuring the people that they can participate in political elections and educational policy-making at the local level.

Bourgeois states exclude workers and their families from meaningful participation in the political processes even as they talk about enfranchising them. Such exclusion is carried through because of the amount of capital required to gain access to the media and the public, to carry on a credible campaign. Voters are given opportunities to vote for delegates to conventions, and political units are defined in terms of territories and interest groups, which control who gets nominated and elected to office.

The state is run by a bureaucracy that does not change much from one term to the next. This bureaucracy carries out the laws enacted by parliaments or congresses and controls the administrative bureaucracy, the courts, and the armed forces. The state uses these administrative arms to carry out mandates from those who possess the wealth and property of the nation. When laws are enacted in the interests of the poorer and working classes, they are often carried out in ways that serve the interests of the dominant classes and their right to remain dominant in the economic, political, and social arenas.

The state has continued to play the role of the intervenor and enforcer in modern times, ensuring the growth and continuation of capitalist relations of property and production. Through its powers of taxation, it has financed huge bureaucracies and armies, which are responsible for protecting special groups and classes. By regulating trade with foreign nations, it has enabled business to seek international markets and low costs and taxes in Third World countries. By emphasizing the need for commerce and transport, it has spent billions on roads and highways, which have become crowded with automobiles. The state's regulation of foreign trade has allowed businessmen to produce their goods in countries where labor is cheap, thus driving millions of production jobs overseas and decimating unions in the United States. Through its control of public administration and the banking system, it has allowed huge amounts of wealth to be siphoned off by unscrupulous members of the business classes.

In modern times, the Germans and Japanese have expanded the role the state plays in guarding the interests of monopoly capitalism.[19] Prior to World War II, other leading capitalist states such as the United States and England had limited the areas in which the government could influence the social and economic activities of the nation. The movement in these countries became one in which the government tried to pose as the representative of all classes in society, even as the power of capital was again making itself felt in the postwar world. More recently it has become clear that the role of the state in modern economies is an expansive one. Monopoly capitalism has been able to generate huge wealth and surpluses, surpluses that were more than domestic markets in any one country could absorb adequately. This meant that all of the advanced capitalist countries were vulnerable to recessions, stagnation, and deep depressions. The trouble was, and is, a shortage of consumer demand, which has led to periodic layoffs and unemployment; and factories have been forced to close. The government, or the state, has become the agency that stimulates the economy by creating demands that will keep the economy on an even keel. Keynesian theories suggested governmental spending in bad times and increasing taxes in good times. But this policy has seldom been followed. Rather, as during the Reagan years, governmental spending increased both in bad times and during the boom that followed the rapid increase in military spending.

Prior to World War I, the capitalist nations were torn between the demands of their internal markets, materials, and investment needs. Two world wars were fought over the division of colonial and market spoils. With the coming of the Russian Revolution in 1917, the doctrine of cordoning off the communist state and surrounding it with military forces and hostile nations became widely accepted. A permanent military force was formed in some of the leading capitalist states to police the world and to make it safe for capitalist investments and influence in Asia, Africa, and South America. This made it easier for states to provide full employment for their economies in ideal circumstances, creating demands that ate up the economic surpluses produced by indigenous capital. Nazi Germany was able to do this on a large scale before World War II by a policy of forced militarization, and the United States did it after the war, when the European world had to be rebuilt and policed by huge armies.

In spite of the wealth generated by capitalist societies, the state has presided over and dealt with ever-growing numbers of poor and unemployed or underemployed populations. In the United States, the wealthiest nation, homeless people live in the streets, and their numbers appear to be growing. Schools continue to be underfunded and seem unable to control the enormous numbers of dropouts and failures they produce in each generation. In order to lessen discontent, the state has given out entitlements and other monies in an attempt to ameliorate the conditions of the destitute, the underemployed or unemployed, and the undereducated. The capitalist class has disagreed over the size and scope of these interventions as they have done since the 1840s, when common schools were debated in the United States. Thus the energies of the underclass and working class have been diverted by these discussions of benefits, and the status quo has been secured and reinforced.

Nevertheless, the pace of industrialization and the frenetic growth of a worldwide economy have increased the need for governmental progams to assist the legions of men and women who are in the labor market or on its fringes. An example of the state's intervening proclivities occurred as World War II was ending.[20] Because of the decade of economic depression that had preceded the war, there was great concern that the return of 11 million soldiers to civilian life would trigger another Great Depression. A *Washington Post* editorial in 1943 looked ahead to a "second Pearl Harbor of peace, not war." This disaster would be more terrible than any wartime battle because the enemy would be the returning soldiers, the returning millions of unemployed workers. There were not enough jobs to go around, and a policy that guaranteed employment was simply not possible. The Delano Committee was convinced that the postwar period would be one of recession or worse, with mass unemployment. To deal with this possibility, the committee recommended that soldiers be delayed in their discharge from the services until jobs were available for them. This plan, however, was never accepted by the Roosevelt administration. The servicemen and their families would never have accepted it, and the committee had to admit that they were unsure when jobs would be available for these men. Still, the problem of how best to keep the returning soldiers off the unemployment lines persisted, and a final solution was to send them back to school for further training. Editorials in 1943 were warning that the returning men would not accept unemployment and poverty docilely, as their parents had done. Congressional committees and the president were worried about what so many millions of Americans might do, especially as they now possessed military skills.

The congressional committees gathered as much data as they could. Most of it pointed to decades of retooling and reconstruction in Europe and Asia, during which time economic depression would be unlikely. But the memories and fears of the 1930s were strong, and planners feared that a big dislocation during the changeover from a wartime to peacetime economy might erode confidence and trigger a downturn.

The final recommendation, of course, was to send these returning veterans to school, to keep them off the unemployment lines, and to pump millions of dollars into the economy as Keynesian economists advised. None of the political or lobbying groups that supported this plan were concerned about education or how these veterans would fit into the institutions of higher learning. Their main concern was to ensure that there would not be a return to the undesirable conditions of the 1930s. Only educators were concerned with the educational impact this legislation would have on them. Only when planners decided to give all veterans four years of training in institutions of higher learning did educators disagree. They believed it would be better to provide subsidization for one year. The next years would depend upon the success or failure of individual students, allowing educators to identify select groups. Yet the colleges were still hungry for students, and the new legislation meant they would have them in abundance. Larger universities had benefitted from the war, training personnel on their campuses and expanding to meet the needs of a massive armed services. Also, research had provided the armed forces with much-needed weaponry, benefiting both parties. Only after the bill was law and the veterans were about to return did leaders in higher education begin to express their concerns about the new educational reforms. James B. Conant, president of Harvard, was distressed because the new law gave support to all veterans without trying to ascertain which of them could benefit most from higher education. His view was that the G.I. Bill should have been directed at only "a carefully selected number of returned veterans." He warned that the new legislation would open a floodgate and that schools would be tempted to admit veterans who did not meet their standards just to earn the tuition. "Because of the G. I. Bill we may find the least capable among the war generation . . . flooding the facilities for advanced education." In 1944, writing in *Collier's Magazine*, he warned that colleges and universities were in danger of being "converted into educational hobo jungles"![21] Of course, all universities actively prepared for the coming of G. I. students, with schools like Harvard getting more than their share of federal funds.

There is evidence, therefore, that the decision to provide higher education for the returning soldiers was triggered not by a desire to establish more equitable relationships and opportunities for Americans but by economic concerns that the returning men would constitute an enormous economic burden. Institutions were ill-equipped to handle the millions who sought entrance after the war. The comments of many educational leaders showed how opposed they were to opening up higher education to prospective students who had little or no experience with colleges or universities. While most of the educators advised against the four-year support program, Congress left little doubt that the returning American soldiers had to be kept off the unemployment lines and out of the labor market. They were to be given access to universities and colleges that had excluded them in the past.

These findings show that educators had a surprisingly negative response to the federal government's efforts to provide returning soldiers with educational opportunities. One of the most sweeping and important educational reforms of the century was accomplished by economic concerns and by political leaders who could not forget the important events of the 1930s. The American soldier was given the economic support he needed to attend college, and millions took advantage of the opportunity and changed the face of higher education (and government). They broke every imaginable enrollment record, more than doubling prewar records, and they proved educational experts like Robert M. Hutchins wrong by taking the more difficult academic courses and completing them successfully. The G. I. Bill democratized higher education by allowing veterans to sit next to students whose family background and income assured them a place in such classrooms. But all this was done by state planners, who once again used the schools to solve social or economic problems. Education became a device for keeping veterans in the classrooms and off the unemployment lines.

THEORETICAL CONSIDERATIONS

If, now, we reconsider this view of the state as the enforcer and intervenor in the social system, another theoretical approach suggests itself. The internal-relatedness thesis changes our focus, helping us to see the state, the economy, the culture, the schools, and other features of society as interconnected parts of an indissoluble entity. No longer are we focusing our attention only upon what causes or connections exist between features of society superstructures and its material base. Now the search is for the inner connections or relations of the parts of this social totality, the ways in which they act and react to one another.[22] The different levels are no longer thought of as discrete phenomena. Changes in one of them presuppose changes in all, and an attempt is made to see the state or the schools as part of a larger social entity. Of course, those who still cling to economic-determination theories of social causality have paid lip service to this idea of reciprocity and interaction between the economic base and superstructures in society. But they have tended to partition reality, confusing their thoughts and language with the social reality they were seeking to study. In the interconnectedness or internal-relatedness theory, the social relations and historical events of a period such as the Great Depression do not invite intervention, per se. But as the state is part of the entire social system that has experienced this traumatic event, we are not surprised that it intervenes. It coexists with the other parts of society and is affected by what happens in each and every one of these parts, just as it influences them when it intervenes or enforces policies that reinforce the status quo.

This idea of interconnectedness appears to be superior to the static ideas of the material base and superstructure we encounter in the Fundamentalist Thesis. Those who embraced it were idealists, in the Hegelian sense, who sought to show a solidarity and harmony between apparently contradictory forces in society. The features of this system insist that none of the constituent parts can be seen or understood apart from one another.

The state cannot be separated analytically from the economy, the culture, the schools, or the family. All of these, as well as other parts, are bound together and cannot logically be unbound. The elements of society are so structured that a change in the state, as an example, would also alter that totality of which the state is a part.

These ideas can be found in the writings of Marx. Again and again he notes that things could only be understood in their relationship to other things in society. In *Grundisse* he criticizes those who would separate out categories such as production, consumption, or distribution of commodities for structural analyses.[23] He notes that production is one and the same as consumption and distribution and that changes in any one of these activities changes all of the elements of the process. A change in the way goods are distributed requires new ways of producing them. Action and interaction are the norm, what one could expect from different parts of an organic whole.

This idea of the organic whole, this category of totality, suggests a push-and-pull process. The intercession of the state helped adversarial classes come together in the schools, in urban centers, and in the industrial workplace. These structures, in turn, changed the configuration and policies of the state. These concepts are opposed to those of empiricism or other theories that seek to discover or make causal judgments about the social structure of modern society. Empiricism assumes that there is an objective world that can be alluded to and understood, however imperfectly. Of course, these understandings are once or twice removed and take place in a world of consciousness or reflection that is not open to empirical verification. Education, family life, culture, and education are some ways in which the world is perceived and made real for the individual. These features of the superstructure are thought of as outgrowths of the economic or material base. In this way of thinking, science will provide us with the laws and understandings that govern human interaction and social systems. Ideologies are considered to be false and distorted views of social reality and need to be exposed. A one-to-one correspondence is assumed between the forms of human consciousness and the object world it seeks to apprehend.

The internal-relatedness theory focuses more on mediation between social institutions and formations and is opposed to the reflective mode so important to empiricists. It focuses on the unseen and misunderstood web of internal relationships that link social systems together. The superstructure is no longer thought of as a secondary phenomenon, separate and apart from the material base. Now the state, the schools, and other features of the superstructure are seen as parts of a totality. No part of social reality should be studied without linking it to the entire social system of which it is merely a segment. Every social relation and event affects every other part of the base and superstructure of society.

In studying the state, we need to understand how the dialectical penetration of the different segments of the social entity interact. Even social theories cannot be separated from the life forms and processes that constitute social systems. The rise of capitalist relations of production have had profound effects on the state and on schooling processes in modern society. Capitalism was predisposed to this schooling activity because it sought to harmonize class conflicts, further scientific advancements, and develop new technologies of production. The educational reformers of the nineteenth century in the United States were successful, in part, because the emergent industrial culture viewed schooling as necessary and desirable. Schooling, however, can now be seen as part of a social system that is inherently unequal and bound up with the exploitation and enslavement of an enormous number of human beings everywhere on this planet. By its very structures and practice, schooling is suffused with concerns about domination and control over students (and teachers), which are inevitably linked to the economic and social systems that have developed in the West. Education (and the family, as we shall see in chapter 4) must thus be viewed as an ideological institution occupied in the inculcation of bourgeois values. Its classroom and organizational structures simulate those of the corporate world, depending for their authority on legal-rational dictates of state governments.

Of course, this thesis of interrelatedness can be undermined. This happens when an attempt is made to salvage rationality, education, history, and science as special cases, despite the presumed insight into the oneness and internal-relatedness of all things. Hegel and Marx held that history was a rational process, guided by the needs and rules of logical thought. But these ideas were couched in the notion that, at some final moment, the rationality of apparently irrational processes would make itself known. Schooling, also, was believed to be a triumph of reason, a giant leap forward. But if these features of modern society are to be seen as outgrowths of capitalistic relations of production and reproduction, we cannot reject the system without rejecting its constituent parts. Marx, of course, believed in the idea of a true science, separate and apart from the social system within which it was established. Yet others have seen science, and education itself, as ideologies produced by modern industrial society because they are useful in establishing new modes of legal-rational authority and maintaining present-day property relations. Only when these ideologies are questioned do they lose their power over the minds of men and women. Schooling can be seen as an effort to inculcate ideas and to control the thoughts of youth, turning them away from ideas of relativism. They must come to regard the state, the nation, the family, and the economy as natural and eternal realities. Thus the idea of death is ignored, as is the notion that, normally, nations and peoples come onto the stage of history and eventually disappear from it. Schooling is dedicated to an ahistorical approach to learning, even as it pretends to teach history. It turns a blind eye to the past, especially when such knowledge could undermine its present-day efforts to sustain and maintain the social relations of educational and material production.

So, schooling and society are to be thought of as structures in an organic totality, with their needs growing out of the productive methods of a given social system. It is not possible to think about our work, schooling or personal problems without paying attention to the economic, social, educational, cultural, and political institutions within which they occur.

This thesis helps us to understand communal and educational experiences in mass schools and societies. It forces us to see struggles among cultures, races, classes, and sexes rather than to see men and women striving to make some sense out of their individual lives. We are thus confronted with still another problem: How can we integrate the individual into these broader constructs of social philosophy? One way is to trust our consciousness, even as we explore the many ways that such consciousness is dominated by ideological and linguistic structures. A teenage boy sitting in a ghetto junior high school twenty years ago might have understood somewhere in his consciousness that he himself was to blame for his continued failure in the schools. He might also see that, if he studied more, he would do better than he was doing—he might even succeed instead of failing. Of course, our arguments would question the accuracy of these perceptions and whether the youngster should blame himself at all for his failures in the classroom. We could point to the segregated nature of his schooling and the impoverished condition of his family. This analysis would not deny the accuracy of his perceptions, but merely deepen them with sociological analysis. It would focus attention on the societal and institutional basis for inequality and failure in mass schools. It would link such failures to the state, the culture, the social relations of production, and so on. And it would allow us to see how we justify inequality of educational and occupational opportunity by making it a function of a youngster's ability to succeed in school. The language and culture of the schools, as we shall see in chapter 3, is one which assures the failure of the poor and racial minorities by confronting them with a curriculum that is alien to them and to their families. On a commonsense level of analysis, the teenager may see his failure as a personal one, accepting the message of the school's authorities. But a broader view, one that emphasizes the interrelatedness of schooling, the state, the culture, and the economy, would place a great deal of the blame on other, unseen social forces.

If our teenager were to realize that his educational experiences were unfair, that they had a race and class bias to them, then he might begin to change some of his ideas. If he thought about the impersonal school building, the large classes, and the often inexperienced or untrained teachers, he might question further the idea that he had been given an equal chance to succeed. He might then come to see that his own efforts probably would not have affected his experiences in school, after all.

Such insights, however, could bring an individual's consciousness into play. It could help our teenager to change the way he saw himself, his family, and his school. It could help him to see through the idea that the individual is completely responsible for what happens to him in school or life, although it could also be used as a crutch, allowing him to blame society and outside forces for his own failure of effort or will. As the boy deepens his understanding of the ways in which socioeconomic class, sexual, and racial formations affect his experiences in classrooms, he can transform his individual awareness of unconscious motivations and begin to grasp those forces that influence his life in unseen and misunderstood ways. Thus the teenager in this example would begin to see how his failing in the junior high school was part of a pattern of failure, a pattern that encompasses generations of urban poor and minority children.

3

Reproduction: Symbolic Violence in Educational Systems

This chapter describes the pedagogical theories of Pierre Bourdieu and his associates and then provides a critique of them. If Bourdieu is correct, then educational systems are characterized by inculcation and a need to reproduce the social relations of production in schools and society. These fulfill schooling's obligation to pass on an arbitrary cultural design, or what Bourdieu calls the *cultural arbitrary*. This term refers to the culture of the dominant classes, which is actually, though not in appearance, based on power. Educational systems cannot escape these social and economic functions: They must reproduce the social relations between classes as they exist in schools and the labor market.[1]

Bourdieu's theories of symbolic violence in educational systems are presented in a series of propositions and glosses that have their own logic and internal consistency. They begin with pedagogic action as the central relationship in the schooling experience, seeing it as the point at which children are regularly subjected to symbolic violence. It is in the act of instruction that an arbitrary cultural scheme is dictated to students by school authorities. It is in the pedagogical act that meaning and values are dictated by agents of the dominant classes on weaker ones. "Every power to exert symbolic violence," Bourdieu writes, "every power which manages to impose meanings and to impose them as legitimate by concealing the power relations which are the basis of its force, adds its own specifically symbolic force to those power relations." This leads to a second thesis about the twofold arbitrariness of pedagogic action: "All pedagogic action is, objectively, symbolic violence insofar as it is the imposition of a cultural arbitrary by an arbitrary power." Bourdieu defines the cultural arbitrary as those communications between teachers and their students which cannot be deduced from any principle, "which are devoid of any sociological or psychological referent."[2] Bourdieu and his associates studied variations in the efficiency of students from different social and scholastic backgrounds and their ability to receive pedagogic communications successfully.[3] They wished to uncover the primary principles underlying the inequalities in academic achievement of children of different social origins and sexes.

Bourdieu's theories sought to explain how cultural and linguistic competencies, or capital, were used to stratify social classes and knowledge in schools. He wished to understand schooling as it was developing during a transition period in France and in other parts of the modern world. Furthermore, his use of a Marxian theoretical framework meant that the schooling of youth was to be closely related to the social, economic, and industrial structures in society. We will deal with these issues when we critique Bourdieu's theories. Here it is enough to say that Bourdieu was interested in the way that society maintained itself and reproduced its cultural and social structures through familial and educational indoctrination.

In *Reproduction in Education, Society and Culture,* Bourdieu and Passeron offer a theory of symbolic violence written in precise language and covering pedagogic action, authority, and work. This was followed by other propositions and glosses about school authority, the educational system, and the reproductive functions of schooling in modern society. Their logic and preciseness stand in contrast to the work of others writing about the schools today. Indeed, the theoretical framework they develop is one of the most comprehensive and stimulating in the social sciences and deserves attention and interest. In dealing further with pedagogic action, the authors provide us with a proposition that serves as their focal point: "the specific productivity of all pedagogic work other than the work of the family is a function of the distance between the habitus it tends to inculcate (scholarly mastery of scholarly language) and the habitus inculcated by the family."[4] *Habitus* is used here to refer to the product of the internalization of the principles of a cultural arbitrary, which was discussed earlier.

Bourdieu and Passeron observe that the schools demand competencies in an arbitrary cultural and linguistic habitus that they themselves cannot provide for the masses of children from working-class and some middle-class families. Such competencies and understandings can be provided only by a child's family and are achieved through a form of linguistic and cultural osmosis rather than in formal classroom lessons. The educational system, therefore, gives an unfair advantage to those who already possess a substantial advantage, by valuing highly the culture and language of elite classes and seeking to reproduce their beliefs, values, and relations in society and the workplace. Thus, educational advantage confirms and legitimizes the positions of those who have inherited cultural and linguistic "capital" from their parents, and the status quo becomes an overwhelming force in the schooling of children. Teachers transmit their versions of this arbitrary culture and language they have learned to imitate and admire, without thinking about what they are doing. Only occasionally do some see the effects their impositional behaviors are having on the self-systems of students.

This emphasis on the beliefs, values, and style of the elite classes forces everyone to value highly such a learning experience and world view. Students who have these competencies and understandings are more highly regarded than those who do not, and the problems of inequality are passed on from one generation to the next. Bourdieu writes elsewhere that students are unequally selected, according to their social origin and sex.[5] Their test scores reflect more than just the consequences of previous training in classrooms, more than just social origins or sex. They represent also the fact that students have not been eliminated, that they are not part of the army of dropouts who are the shame of schooling in the industrial, capitalist nations.

These ideas suggest that Bourdieu and his associates believe that the concepts of linguistic capital (learned at home) and the degree of selection are capable of explaining, in a systematic way, the relations between teachers and pupils. Furthermore, given the demand that students meet minimum requirements of acculturation and language proficiency, the middle and working classes who reach institutions of higher learning have necessarily undergone "more stringent selection processes than their upper class" counterparts.[6] In short, Bourdieu and his co-workers believe that the influence of language shows itself in the earliest years of family life and schooling, when linguistic capital is used by teachers to measure and assess their students' competencies and worth. These influences on a youngter's schooling career "never cease to be felt," according to the authors.

But language is not the only form of communication in classrooms. Pedagogic action also provides, along with richer and poorer vocabularies, a "complex set of categories, so that the capacity to decipher and manipulate complex structures, whether logical or aesthetic, depends partly on the complexity of the language and world views transmitted by the family."[7] The cultural boundaries of an individual's life are set by the beliefs, values, and understandings of the world, which are learned in interaction with parents and family members. Educational dropouts can be expected to increase in number as one moves toward students in socioeconomic classes most distant from the arbitrary language and habitus of the schools, that is, from the language of ideas and schooling. These ideas provided Bourdieu with a sociocultural perspective for understanding an individual student's success or failure in school. Such success or failure could be measured as a relationship between a student's possession of cultural and linguistic capital, as identified by his or her father's occupation and his or her level of academic achievement.

Bourdieu is particularly concerned with the disparity in achievement scores between men and women in French institutions of higher learning. He notes a constant superiority of men over women and relates these to a systematic condition wherein women were streamed into lower-status careers while men were encouraged to study medicine, science, and law. His studies indicate that women, principally through the process of initial streaming, were victimized by social origin and sex. The type of elementary or secondary school they attended predetermined their educational fate, much as the fate of minority children was determined by their forced incarceration in urban ghetto schools. Subsequent learnings and career choices assured women of less opportunity for success than their male counterparts. Still, Bourdieu notes, the structure of selection survivors was constantly changing according to new criteria governing elimination. This tended to weaken the relationship between social origin and linguistic competence. Nevertheless, the sons of senior executives were on the top of the university system, studying high-status disciplines. Social origin, with its initial socialization and learning patterns, could not be considered as a factor capable of explaining every attitude, opinion, and practice in an individual's life. The constraints of the selection system had to be understood by examining particular educational systems at different moments in their history and development.

It should be noted, too, that Bourdieu describes an array of social characteristics and associations that defined the first experiences and conditions of children from different social classes. He does this in order to better understand the different probabilities that various educational experiences would have for them and the significance for individuals in different social classes of finding themselves in situations of greater or lesser prestige and status. It was highly improbable that children of manual workers, sons of laborers, would study Latin and Greek in schools; it was more probable that they would have to work, if they decided to stay in school and pursue a career in higher education.

Bourdieu's work has theoretical implications that deserve further attention. Again and again, the authors speak of the arbitrary habitus of schooling and of a type of pedagogy that affects the way children see themselves, their families, and their possibilities for educational and occupational careers. They relate these ideas to the social classes in France and examine them within the context of the social selection system of schools and society. These ideas allude to a theory of classes that focuses upon dominant and subordinate groups, on elitism as it has evolved in modern-day France. To the authors, the pedagogy and culture schools transmit to students of middle- and working-class children is a form of symbolic violence, a way in which methods of instruction appear to mirror practices in the social and economic world.

Their analysis of pedagogic action is framed within the context of still another postulate: the process of social reproduction of the existing culture and society and its social relations of power. The weakness in such postulates can be a confirmation of previously held ideas of class struggle and conflict. Still, these postulates and glosses are some of the few that attempt to tie in an analysis of schooling with the political, economic, and social class structures of society. They relate schooling's culture to the structural and relational features of adult life and show how educational systems perpetuate cultures by their practices and arbitrary assumptions about knowledge, life, and children.

The functions of inculcation, communication, selection, and legitimation lead to a maintenance of the status quo, to a maintenance of the social and power relations between the classes. In this sense, schooling is seen as a profoundly conservative institution, à la Durkheim. The cultural arbitrary, as the authors refer to that which is designated as valid knowledge and practice in schools, is labelled "symbolic violence" and is manifested in the authoritarian nature of instruction and the adoption of the crudest forms of coercion and control. Modern industrial society, more than others before it, must seek a legitimation for the social inequality and transmission of power and privilege from one generation to the next.

PEDAGOGIC AUTHORITY AND WORK

It may prove helpful to discuss further some other aspects of pedagogic action as it has been developed in these theories of symbolic violence. Whenever possible, the authors advise, attention should be paid to the structure of pedagogic authority implied in the definition of pedagogic action. This refers to the power that schools have to exert symbolic violence in ways that accentuate their legitimate nature in legal-rational society, concealing the powers that established them in the first instance. According to Max Weber, legitimate culture is endowed with traditional, charismatic, or legal-rational authority. These forms are neither more nor less than the dominant cultural arbitrary of the moment, in the language of Bourdieu and Passeron. They sensitize us to the symbolic actions and practices of the arbitrary habitus in schools and assure us that these can subsist only when they reinforce predispositions in society itself. In France, the right and power to administer symbolic violence through pedagogical action is given to state and private academic institutions, which can and will use their authority to inculcate the cultural arbitrary legitimately.

Similarly, Bourdieu defines pedagogic work as the requirements that pedagogic institutions must follow as they reproduce the principles of the cultural arbitrary. This cultural arbitrary is imposed by groups and classes who are considered worthy of reproduction because of their power and reputation in society and because they have apparently delegated to a neutral agency (schools) the authority needed to reproduce it. Pedagogic work can be measured by the degree to which it succeeds or fails in its function of inculcation, of reproducing the existing culture and social relations of production.[8]

The authors' definition of pedagogic work goes further in suggesting that the methods and length of inculcation are important sources of power for pedagogic authorities and institutions. Educators are the ones who define when a person has had enough schooling, enough competence in the arbitrary habitus of the schools, enough training to be considered an educated person worthy of graduation. In addition, the authors point out that pedagogic work is a substitute for physical constraint: it forces children to sit and attend by bringing sanctions against those who fail to accept and internalize the cultural arbitrary. Pedagogic work is a hidden form of coercion and constraint, a symbolic violence that forces youngsters to sit in classrooms long after they have dropped out intellectually and emotionally. The longer the process of enforced schooling and the more complete the arbitrariness of pedagogic action and schoolwork become, the more schooling is able to conceal the truth of the arbitrary habitus it seeks to impose on students. Every movement of the dominant culture is toward legitimacy, attempting to exclude other forms of language and culture from the culture from the acculturating process of schooling. Those who find themselves excluded from the benefits of schooling are subjected to a symbolic force that questions their self-worth and competence.[9] Compulsory education forces the dominated classes to recognize and accept the schools' version of knowledge and know-how. Pedagogic work produces a primary habitus, characteristic of a group or class that controls the identification and transmission of valid knowledge and behavior from one generation to the next. As in pedagogic action, the degree of effective pedagogic work is a function of the distance between the habitus it inculcates and that implied by previous pedagogic action from the family or community. The success of a student depends upon her family and preschool years, even though schools perpetuate the ideology that all children start their schooling on an equal footing. The acquisition of language, skills in solving everyday problems, kinship relations, logical forms of thinking, and worldly perspectives are mastered during these formative years. These cultural beliefs, attitudes, values, self-concepts, and perspectives are symbolic in nature and tie one to a particular class in society, predisposing children unequally toward a symbolic mastery of the pedagogic action and work in classrooms.

EDUCATIONAL SYSTEMS

Every educational system has to produce and reproduce the structural and relational conditions necessary to the exercise of its primary function of inculcation. Every one of them needs to fulfill its social function of reproducing the cultural arbitrary of both the school and the society that funds and operates it. All educational systems must reproduce the relations between classes that exist in the social relations of material production.[10] In the final section of their theory of symbolic violence, the authors pose the question: What must an educational system be in order for it to be able to create and maintain the institutional conditions that will allow it to produce a habitus and to assure its misrecognition by students and teachers alike? They found that it was not possible to reduce this question to a historical search for the social conditions of a particular educational system. Going beyond Durkheim, who sought to understand the nature of educational systems by looking backward toward the early Christian habitus and Greco-Roman heritage,[11] they looked also at the forms that schooling and society adopted as they tried to solve the problems of the past. Bourdieu and his associates believed that only by examining such structures could they come to see and understand the social forces that gave rise to different historical situations and social processes such as high-speed industrial production, the development of the division of labor and the autonomization of intellectual centers and practices, the development of a strong demand for manufactured goods, and so on. Only then could they examine these structures and their influence on the ongoing life forces in society.

Progress made by an educational system such as paying teachers, organizing and training them systematically, standardizing educational organization over a wide area, and instituting examinations and civil service status was all part of the bureaucratic establishment and institutionalization of pedagogic work. Durkheim identified the medieval university as the first educational system in Europe because it had within its structure evaluation methods that validated the results of inculcation (the diploma). This evaluation component was Durkheim's primary consideration because it united the pedagogic action of inculcation and forced it into a more homogeneous, standardized pattern. Weber might have added that such educational systems were also characterized by a cadre of specialized personnel whose training, recruitment, and careers were controlled by the institution and who found, in the educational system, a way of maintaining their claim to a monopoly of legitimate inculcation of the arbitrary habitus or culture of the school and society.

As educational systems cannot perform their essential function of inculcation unless they produce and reproduce the structural and relational conditions for their own pedagogical work, a habitus as homogeneous and durable as possible in as many students and teachers as possible is necessary. The system's external functions of cultural and social reproduction force it to produce a habitus as close as possible to the cultural arbitrary that it was funded and mandated produce.

The need to assure homogeneous and orthodox schoolwork forces the educational system to move toward standardized training for both teachers and their students. Standardized curriculum, pedagogical methods, and tests are used to measure students against one another. The tools of teaching that the educational system uses are not only aids in the performance of pedagogic action but also ways to limit the goals, perspectives, and content of classroom work. Textbooks, syllabuses, manuals—all have the effect of unifying what is taught in different classrooms by different teachers. The need to codify and systematize the pedagogic communication and school culture is conditioned by the demands for homogeneity and orthodoxy in increasingly strained mass societies. All learning in educational systems is done within the framework of an essentially apprenticeship system in which the student is socialized out of his ignorant condition over a period of many years. This binds the graduates, teachers, and students to the educational system and to the economic and social system.

The institutionalization of pedagogic action is characterized by an obsessive concern for self-reproduction. There is an inadequacy of research training and inquiry methods up and down the grade system. There is a programming of the norms of research and the objects of inquiry so that the interests of the status quo are served. Educational systems are relatively autonomous institutions monopolizing the legitimate use of symbolic violence and serving groups or classes whose cultural arbitrary they reproduce.

HISTORICAL PERSPECTIVES

There is no intention here to present Bourdieu's ideas in their entirety. It would take volumes to discuss all the nuances of his position on the educational system and its functions in the modern capitalist state. The purpose here is to examine pedagogic action and authority in mass educational systems as they have evolved during the recent past. Doing so requires that we look at the historical record from which many of these ideas developed, in the hope that they will provide insight into these ideas and the urban and industrial structures within which they took root. The problems of individual and social disorganization that accompanied the end of World War II will be our preliminary focus. The reasons may become evident as we move along, but it seems important to say here that the best way to develop deeper insights into the structural relations of state institutions such as the family and the schools is to relate them to specific historical processes and events.

Some sense of the times can be gained by examining the great leap in technology that followed the war and the Marshall Plan, much of it developed in response to military and economic needs and the looming Cold War. Here was an atmosphere of systemic hostilities and change, with the people of France turning more and more to Marxist ideas, with large socialist and communist parties striving for political attention and power. The world seemed to be divided into those who wished to return to the world as it had existed before the war and those who did not. People in the colonies now demanded greater autonomy and independence and a say in their political and economic destinies. Policy was developed within the context of a shrinking capitalist market that made it seem as though communism was gaining the upper hand in France and elsewhere in Europe and Asia. Indigenous forces opposed to the old colonialism joined hands and created a world in which armaments were welcomed, whatever their source. The French economy, with its constantly shrinking horizons and military budgets, was in trouble through much of this period. Communist governments seemed to cherish a vision of the world in which there were no capitalist states. Of course, this feeling was also part of the anti-Communist sentiment that tried successfully to isolate the Communist party.

Many on both sides of this conflict had spent the war years in an uneasy alliance. But this was quickly forgotten by the leaders of both sides, and the world was seen, more and more, as balancing on the brink of a revolutionary era. Class conflict and class struggle dominated the intellectual climate of France. No country seemed to be in a more precarious condition than France and, perhaps, Italy. The struggle between those who wished to maintain or change the old order became a part of the era's character and tended to control the thinking of people in France and elsewhere. The pressure to maintain or destroy the world that had existed prior to World War II led both sides to rearm themselves and their allies.

Bourdieu and his associates were old enough to have felt the full effects of these social and intellectual upheavals. They studied during a time when France was still threatened by the communists and when the Algerian and Vietnam wars were fresh in the minds of many. Their work took on the notion of class struggle and symbolic violence, of change and conflict between people from different social origins and sexes, from factions competing for scarce resources and knowledge.

Some demography without statistics may be in order. The world population continued to grow at an unprecedented rate, as did the number of people living in a culture of poverty on the edges of the industrial world. Whole continents flirted with revolution and counterrevolution, and war became a constant of the times. Small wonder that the thinkers of this era focused on problems of equality and conflict, emphasizing the difficulties that were associated with the working class and its status and condition in France and the West and, increasingly, the lack of political freedom in the communist countries. If to this is added the fact that many of the former colonial nations refused to submit to the yoke again, it then becomes clear why France was thus divided into opposing camps.

The defeats in the colonial wars provided the initial stimulus for immigration from Africa and Asia and forced the educational system in France to deal with students from foreign linguistic and cultural backgrounds. The institutionalization of social mobility came more slowly in France, but it did inch forward. With it came an increased orientation toward consumerism. People seemed inclined to work in order to obtain mass-produced commodities; industrial production became more sophisticated. Unlike the United States, however, France suffered economic setbacks and high levels of unemployment, further limiting opportunities for the students and workers from the old colonies.

While it is true that France was forced to fight a losing campaign in Algeria and Vietnam, she was able to stay out of further military adventures and associated with the NATO alliance. Being a nuclear power, she was only too aware of the destructiveness of the new weapons and their ability to destroy humankind. In the meantime, a second leap forward in technology and productive capacities changed the balance of forces in the world once more, coming to France later than it did to America and Japan. A competitive society seemed to encourage innovation and initiative workers more than did its socialist counterparts. Certainly one of the outcomes was a more robotized, computerized society in which the power of productive workers was curtailed. This foreshadowed new problems of production and adjustment for people and seemed to make military solutions to world problems less feasible, at least as far as the two superpowers were concerned. The world needed to find new ways to live together in peace, and Europe was able to join together in a common market and defense system.

The changes during this period included the breakdown of labor-intensive industries and the exportation of jobs to Third World nations where labor was cheaper. This revolution provided a social transformation in the relations between business and working-class communities in France, with the recent immigrants from the colonies caught in the middle. The workers were well-organized in unions and seemingly entrenched in the 1950s. They seemed better organized than businessmen, but unable or unwilling to force the educational system to deal effectively with their own children or with the children of the immigrants. Opportunities for students and workers were limited by consistently high rates of failure and unemployment, which had the effect of keeping wages low. Yet many were confident of the future and of an eventual triumph of egalitarian, Marxist ideas.

Toward the end of the 1960s, technology and the practices of world capitalism began to sap the energies and strength of labor and its unions. Unskilled workers found themselves in difficult conditions, and those from the former colonies seemed to bear the brunt of these developments. They seemed least able to compete for jobs and educational training. The communist and socialist unions seemed to have a brief flicker of success in 1968, as students led workers in a national work-stoppage. During this period Bourdieu and his associates studied the educational system to learn why it had failed so miserably in its attempts to educate children from the former colonies and from the working classes of France. The old institutional structures of the educational system now seemed to be empty forms that were unable to deal with the problems of everyday life; they appeared to children and their parents as rigid constructs that could not, or would not, change themselves in order to serve more effectively the children of the immigrants and urban poor.

A CRITIQUE

Our critique must begin with an analysis of the concept of *reproduction*. The idea is a biological one, implying that educational systems and societies are social organisms with functions mirroring those of the higher animals. This leads to a sterile functionalism, which has as a major unspoken supposition the assumption of orderliness in the educational and social worlds. Functionalism, of course, refers to a general set of theories or models that include the following categories: a social formation must itself against the scourges of starvation and exposure to the elements; it must satisfy its basic, primitive need to survive. Once this has been accomplished, secondary needs such as sexual gratification, reproduction, and family structures can be arranged. Lastly, social formations and ideologies that move persons to cooperate in the social relations of material production need to be put in place. These categories reflect the needs that animals have in the empirical world, and they are conveyed in the language of the everyday world, of ideological thought. This idea that the social world can best be understood by conceptualizing it as a biological organism has historical roots. It was popular during the period from 1850 to 1914, when the object world seemed to be knowable simply by paying close attention to its functions and outer appearances. Such approaches to social knowledge, such as Durkheim's theories of mechanical and organic solidarity, tried to understand social relations by referring them to the universal needs of living animals or organisms. Society was seen as an entity that possessed the same needs, drives and impulses as individuals. Of course, theorists who used this functionalist perspective came to see that there were some social agencies that seemed to have no apparent reason for being, no function in the larger scheme of things. Others noted that some social agencies had many functions. Finally, there were social institutions that were labeled dysfunctional by theorists because they seemed to press against the presumed needs of society to meet their most basic requirements. A recurring feature of such theories is that of misrecognition or unconscious motivations: the individual is seen as a person who cannot fully understand the ways in which outside or unseen forces affect his life. In Bourdieu's theories, this becomes misrecognition. Individuals interact with one another, but they are unable to see the hidden force that structures their encounters. They are unable to see the power that supports the legitimate authority in educational systems and the labor market.

These theories hinge on the idea that people who attend schools are unaware of the arbitrary requirements of such institutions. The state is seen as a primary agency of reproduction, a structural entity whose task is to recreate the social, economic, and cultural relations of material production. It is responsible for carrying out this function and for doing it in ways that have the support of the dominant forces in society. Marxists like Bourdieu often overemphasize the power that the state or the schools have in reproducing the social relations of production from one generation to the next. Economic realities often accomplish this task better, teaching the poor to keep their place without stirring up the class conflicts associated with the work of state agencies. Families teach youngsters who they are and how they should see the world long before they ever attend school. They learn these lessons in daily living, and the schools are asked only to validate these original understandings. Still schooling is not as focused and conflict ridden as Bourdieu would have us believe. Often, the family and educational systems send children congruent messages that confuse and defuse the natural anger of children. Less often, families send children messages that oppose those of the schools and prepare youth for a more conscious struggle against their oppressed conditions.

In Bourdieu's world, children and teachers are unconscious robots who cannot understand what they are doing in their classrooms. Even if we accept the ideas of Freudian unconsciousness, or a Lacanian variation of the de-centered individual, we cannot accept the idea of a total lack of consciousness. Indeed, psychoanalysis postulates that the individual possesses some free will, although an overwhelming part of his existence is governed by unconscious impulses. Bourdieu's teachers and students are persons with no free will. They cannot influence what happens between them and are fated to submit to the symbolic violence of state educational systems without thought or comprehension. Bourdieu seems to echo conservatives like Talcott Parsons of Harvard University. In the theoretical formulations of both, the world is peopled with individuals who are controlled by social structures. Parson's people don't seem to be capable of conscious action, while Bourdieu's are completely unable to understand what pedagogical actions are really about. Yet we know that the state has been an arena which has tried to mediate, as much as possible, the conflicting demands of the social classes under its authority. Mostly, it has reflected the arbitrary culture and habitus of the dominant classes. But there have been exceptions. In the previous chapter we alluded to the broadening of educational opportunity that accompanied the end of World War II and the passage of the G. I. Bill of Rights. Also, efforts by educational systems to provide remedial programs for immigrant and retarded children indicate that there is greater conflict beneath the bureaucratic surface than Bourdieu's theories permit.

Functionalist solutions become too predisposed to an orderly world in which everything can be explained in systematic propositions. Yet the world has moved far from such views. Theoretical physics has taught us relativity, and the broadening of our cultural horizons in urban settings around the globe has introduced this concept into social thought. Only now are we becoming aware of how complex simple acts of perceptions are, once sufficient knowledge is gained by researchers. The idea that a required function of social systems might automatically call forth agencies and ideological thought that answer those needs seems simplistic indeed. Making the individual an object in the classroom costs Bourdieu and his associates any opportunity to explain the conscious behavior that teachers and students do utilize, now and then. The idea of the pedagogic act as one of symbolic violence can be challenged. It can also be seen as the effort of state ideological apparatuses such as the family, the church, the state, and its schools to work in harmony, strengthening the social bonds of society. Exploitation of certain classes surely exists. But so do social solidarity-producing behaviors. It is this cohesiveness that gives to social formations the mutual consent one can observe in caste systems in India or in some advanced capitalist states. It permits individuals to become devout patriots, religious supporters of churches and temples, or dependable workers and family men and women. But even here, simple categories may break down in the empirical world. A family may be designated as working class by Bourdieu and his associates because of the occupation of the father. But middle-class values may predominate at home because of the social biography of the mother or because the father is upwardly mobile and consciously striving to better himself.

Nevertheless, functionalism has an affinity for the structural features of Marxist thought even as it ignores its respect for historical specificity. Its basic assumption, that because needs can be articulated for society they will call into existence institutions that satisfy such needs, is itself not a forceful argument. It is not specific in its delineation of how such needs are satisfied by different social and economic agencies and what conflicts arise in such agencies. Still, it can be asked in the last instance:

Even if a need for reproduction could be identified, why should the satisfaction of such a need be given to schools or the state? Maybe all such talk of social needs should be put to one side because they are necessarily ideological in their forms and language.

Bourdieu's theories assume that the dominant classes in society have enough insight and knowledge of their interests to assure them. Yet the recent history of capitalism suggests that this is probably not so. In this century two world wars have been fought, and communism has had a meteoric rise and sudden collapse in Eastern Europe. Surely this was not in the best interests of Western capitalism or Russian socialism, yet these events happened. Bourdieu's theories suggest that working-class parents are unable to make any meaningful changes in the practices and conditions in state agencies and schools, and much evidence supports this view. Yet the state's recognition of union rights, welfare, health insurance, and social security suggests states also possess a mediation function that Bourdieu and his associates have ignored.

Agreeing with Louis Althusser, Bourdieu sees educational systems as one of the places where the class war is raging, as a place where the dominant classes control and socialize the working classes into accepting their places in the social relations of material production.[12] Again and again he writes of education's contribution to the reproduction of the social and educational relations of production and the symbolic relations between the classes. Educational agencies are seen as instruments that perpetuate existing social and economic patterns, as extremely conservative forces in modern society. They accomplish this by requiring from pupils a cultural and linguistic ability that they themselves cannot convey, an ability that only a few in the dominant classes possess as a consequence of their family backgrounds. Following Althusser further, Bourdieu specifies that the educational system has superseded the Church as the dominant agency of inculcation. It is in the classroom that children learn what they must know in order to survive in a society of exploiters and exploited populations.

THE DISSOLVED INDIVIDUAL

Bourdieu's theories dissolve the individual, removing him from consciousness and an ability to influence what is happening to him in the classroom. But this individual is far removed from what Marx envisioned or what we have become accustomed to in humanist literature. He is removed from any understanding or free will during the pedagogic act. His insights, and those of his teachers, are those of persons who can only misrecognize what is happening between them. The experience of children in schools is seen as a social and political one, with actors being unable to understand the hidden functions and powers that structure the schooling situation. Also, Bourdieu sees only social and class conflict in educational systems, ignoring others like Durkheim and Althusser, who saw schools as ideological state institutions, as social solidarity-producing agencies with many of the same functions as families and churches. The act of teaching can be viewed as one of social cohesion, providing both the teacher and student with social knowledge they can use in their everyday lives together. It can be understood as part of an inculcation process that has its early stirrings in the family and church or temple. Schools may have linguistic and cultural habituses alien to the poorer classes, but they also possess an ideological message that calls upon them to provide instruction for the retarded, to ameliorate the inequalities of capitalism even as they appear to fail miserably in practice. That some individuals do make it through the long years of tedious inculcation seems to indicate that these exceptions to the norm need further attention. Also, an individual's idea of success or failure will often be determined by his original place in the social scale. Often such success can be missed, because it is merely one step on the long ladder of social status gradations. Bourdieu recognized these problems, treating them as exceptions to the class war that was being waged in the schools. Yet Gramsci showed that a person's experiences in the social world were both individualistic and sociohistorical in nature.[13] The individual found herself placed in a particular time and place and faced a world that had been in existence before she was born. But she was also an individual who could transcend both linguistic and class heritages, experiencing both the conflict and the cohesion that are part of the social experience.

Bourdieu's idea that people's identities are determined by their relations to the material modes of production is a Marxian one. But it ignores cultural and religious attitudes that also exert a strong influence on an individual's self-concept and understanding of his socioeconomic condition. For Bourdieu, the free-willed person is a myth. The individual is capable only of misrecognition of the daily reality he or she experiences in classrooms. Theoretical postulates are used, but they assign meaning to classroom events different from those the actors themselves would give were they asked to reflect on them. The work of education is seen as one that commits symbolic violence on the children of the immigrant, the middle classes, and the poor. But these acts of regimentation and control can help disparate individuals to come together as citizens of a nation, especially if the differing groups or classes internalize their places in the social pyramid and strive to succeed within that limiting structure. Here an observer can see conflict and oppression or cohesion and socialization, depending upon the original postulates of his philosophical orientations.

A second area of concern is Bourdieu's separation of theory from practice. Unlike empirical theorists and researchers, who put forth postulates and glosses that can then be tested in real classrooms or workplaces, Bourdieu and his associates insist that, because the teachers and students in educational settings misrecognize what is really happening between them, testable propositions are impossible. They proclaim their theories to be scientific even though these formulations do not correspond to what is happening in classrooms anywhere in the world. The propositions are true because they have a logic and an internal consistency that protect them from empirical proofs or falsifications. For Bourdieu and his associates, theories are conceptual frames that talk about empirical events but for which only inferential evidence can be deduced.

Bourdieu's ideas about social theories are supported by Marxist traditions, which often felt that the variables associated with social interaction were so numerous as to rule out empirical approaches. Their rejection of empiricism forced them to rely upon unstated coherence theories as the validation of their postulates and glosses. Logical compatibility became the criterion for validating different findings and insights. A second form of coherence theory lay in the assumption that theories were comprehensive and needed to include as much as possible of the world in which people lived. This made it unnecessary for them to justify thoughts by referring them to concrete historical events, as these were being misunderstood by actors who could not see the hidden forces at work in their situations. Thus Bourdieu can use the idea of misrecognition to explain away contradictory, behaviors of students and teachers, who seldom see the conflict beneath their associations but often see social solidarity-building activities occurring in their classrooms. Bourdieu's propositions can never be directly challenged or validated because they have no counterpart in the interaction that occurs between teachers and students in schools. The difference between scientific theories and ideologies, mentioned in chapter 1, is that science recognizes the problems inherent in its own use of language and ideas while ideology presents itself as a true representation of what is happening in the world on an everyday basis.

Still, the problems with Bourdieu's theories go beyond these difficulties. How can an observer know, as a fact, that symbolic violence is being perpetrated on a student if that student sees the interaction as beneficial, as a socially positive experience? Surely some pedagogical work can be seen in this way or can include both the conflict and the cohesion at the same moment, in the same interaction. If theory is not anchored in empirical reality of some sort, it may be very much removed from what is happening to teachers and children in classrooms. Logical coherence is to be commended, of course, but it is not enough. Theory needs to be grounded, to some degree, on more than internal consistencies. Consistent accounts of pedagogic actions as solidarity-producing acts can be generated as easily as the symbolic violence Bourdieu produced, even as we agree with him that violence appears to have the upper hand in the pedagogic act. Both of these approaches may have merit, or at least they may present us with insights into the complexity and ambivalence at the root of so many human reactions to social experience. It is possible that the functions of educational systems are complex and that there is no one way to account for their outcomes. At best, Bourdieu's theories can be seen as plausible explanations for many of the practices and outcomes he and his associates uncovered in their studies of French education. But their theories seem to have been limited by their initial assumptions of conflict.

To repeat, the everyday happenings between teachers and students in classrooms is a comedy of errors for Bourdieu and his associates. They produce only misrecognition of the symbolic violence being perpetrated there. The teachers' or students' understandings of classroom experiences are evidences of false consciousness, myths, and ideologies that keep them from recognizing what is really happening. Only Marxists like Bourdieu can provide insights into the truth that lies behind these images and interactions, which departs from his own declared goal of placing educational theory on a more scientific basis. This separation of theory from concrete experiences in schools and classrooms is a problem for Bourdieu, inherited from his Marxist tradition. It is rooted in the fact that Marx's major predictions did not come true. The working classes in the advanced industrial countries did not overthrow capitalism. In fact, during World War I they chose to abandon their international ties, fighting under the banners of nationalism. These failures forced others to reinterpret Marx's ideas, and his concept of false consciousness came into widespread use. They helped to explain why the industrial proletariat failed to play its assigned historic role, why it has appeared to be oblivious to its own best interests time and time again.

EPISTEMOLOGICAL PROBLEMS

In developing theories of pedagogic action and educational systems, Bourdieu and his associates moved away from empirical observations of social relations in classrooms. They sought to avoid the problems of knowledge and knowing that were implicit in symbolic violence and an ideological interpretation of classroom realities. Therefore, they defined pedagogic action as, logically, an act of symbolic violence perpetrated through the enforcement of a cultural arbitrary. Yet to call attention to this feature of pedagogic action and the misrecognition that accompanies symbolic violence is not to dispose of epistemological problems. The ability to think about educational production seems to imply an ability to correct misrecognitions through the use of reflection. The problems can be stated in the following manner: Are Bourdieu's ideas able to explain all of the facets of pedagogic action, or do they merely describe a part of it? In terms of the effects of such actions on teachers and students, there seem to be other, more benign effects. The question of adequacy hounds Bourdieu's concepts, leaving the reader to decide whether they are capable of grasping more than a part of the experiences they claim to describe. The problem of how human beings can know the world in which they live is an important one. Bourdieu does not give an account of this problem. Words and ideas are used to develop his theories of pedagogic action logically, without ever taking into account the problems that come about when social reality is changed into linguistic and ideational constructs. As to symbolic violence, Bourdieu seems to deduce his notions from the real effects he sees in French education and society. His concept of misrecognition seems to echo ideas of false consciousness and appears to cover up those aspects of pedagogic action that are seen as positive, solidarity-producing effects. Still, symbolic violence appears to be real enough, and its effects are everywhere apparent. How can the forced teaching of alien linguistic and cultural arbitraries lead to anything else? Misrecognition seems to be one way to describe this situation, but the yearning for assimilation and access into industrial labor markets may also have a place here.

Bourdieu's theories have their greatest force when they speak of the symbolic violence inherent in pedagogic action and work. Children's levels of violence will depend upon the class positions of their parents and the language and cultural categories taught in the preschool years. These in turn are related to the history of social formations, to the modes of material production in the ascendency at any given moment in time. Yet Bourdieu's theories are overly structural and functional in their orientations and free of historical determinations. Like the hidden powers that establish and operate schools, these structures and their symbolic violence are ahistorical forms that occur in any and all social formations. The ideas of teachers, students, and parents are ideological in nature and provide a misleading and false understanding of what is really happening to them in schools.

Bourdieu's work also suffers from the objectification of the individual in educational systems. The subject-object dialectic associated with Descartes is abandoned. The individual who thinks, feels, and changes the social world through knowledge is no longer in evidence. Now teachers, students, and parents are objects moved about by unseen forces that direct the work of educational production. The old idea of the individual as the center of social life and experience is abandoned. The new person cannot understand what is really happening; mental capabilities cannot assure that sufficient knowledge to act intelligently can be acquired, as all experiences must be transformed into language, into ideological constructs. The teacher, student, and parents in Bourdieu's world are subjected to mimetic structures that control them. They do not, and cannot, change their destinies or the history of the educational systems in which they work and learn. Individuals are part of a world they did not make and cannot understand, except through misrecognition and ideology. They are destined to fill their positions in the given educational and social-relations structures of modern society.

The inculcation processes of the pedagogic action begin, however, in the family. There neonates develop many-sided and conflictual natures of themselves, which will be discussed further in chapter 4. Here we want to point out that infants make the passage from animals to human beings, from sensations and needs to language and a recognition of society and their places in it. Children come to see themselves as the center of experience, the people who initiate much of the action that occurs around them. This process places children in an ideological mode. They come to see and understand themselves by recognizing the linguistic categories others use to describe and identify them. They come to misrecognize these words as their selves or, as Bourdieu might say, they misrecognize or confuse these words with their own inner cores. The parents with whom children identify are idealized versions of persons, who seem to have no other function or desire than to minister to the needs of their children. This misrecognition is the essence of ideology and governs the consciousness, actions, and experiences of children and others around them. Yet these earliest pedagogic acts contain more than symbolic violence, if you will. They also contain a bonding of individuals with nurturing others and an acceptance of social solidarity-producing outcomes that are the cement of modern societies.

SUMMARY AND CONCLUSION

Bourdieu and his associates developed a theory of symbolic violence that sought to examine the reproductive functions of schooling in modern society. They studied the arbitrary characteristics and practices of educational systems and their effects on children from different social origins and sexes. Individual consciousness and understanding of ongoing classroom experiences were ignored because they were misrecognitions of the power hidden behind the symbolic violence of the pedagogic act. Yet these perspectives made it impossible for researchers to operationalize their hypotheses and concepts. Findings could not be developed to validate their theoretical formulations, because such findings could not be observed or replicated in ongoing classroom activities. The teachings of educational systems were seen as arbitrary in their content and forms. Because these teachings were imposed on children by the state and the dominant classes the state represented, their habitus was arbitrary and could not be derived from principles of logic in social science research.

Pedagogic action was based on ideological ways of thinking, ways that caused individuals to misrecognize what was happening to them in classroom situations. But Bourdieu and his associates failed to attend to the solidarity-producing features of pedagogic action and ideologies, nor did they explain why Durkheim and many psychoanalysts saw pedagogic action as "social cement," which initiated individuals into social formations such as schools, economic organizations, and society. Their propositions and glosses of pedagogic action were evolved from logical deduction and could not be modified or verified by empirical research.

Still, the primary fault in this elaborate theory of schooling is their denial of the human factor in schooling's practice and history. This causes them to embrace a functionalist and deterministic approach to educational systems. Schooling is seen as an ongoing set of interactions and structures. The individual who reflects, speaks, and causes things to happen is absent. In his place is the individual as object. Now individuals do not make their histories. Rather, the histories of significant others and mimetic structures compel individuals to march down a predetermined path. Researchers were urged by these social scientists to study the social relations of educational production rather than the subjects who were part of such pedagogic action. The place and functioning of the individual was determined by his class position. In these theories, conscious human choice and insights were denied to individuals. Bourdieu denied free will to teachers, students, or parents, seeing them as the bearers of class ideologies and distorted understandings of their true conditions in schools and society. Thus, class determinism replaced the idea of free agency for actors, forcing out any empirical validation for their propositions. Bourdieu's research and theories were distinguished by a coherence theory that sought to validate their propositions by relying on internal consistency alone. This focus on underlying structures of educational production was accomplished at the expense of the teacher and her students, who often saw pedagogical work in more positive ways.

Bourdieu and his associates also found that inequality, which was seen at all levels of education, was not merely the result of the examination system or streaming practices. It was also a consequence of class differences in linguistic abilities and understandings, in cultural and linguistic capital.[14] The ways in which cultural reproduction in schools and society were accomplished were related to the class war and the need to maintain the power and privileges of dominant classes from one generation to the next. The imposition of an arbitrary habitus favorable to the dominant classes accentuated the symbolic violence component of pedagogic action, raising important questions. The use of socioeconomic classes in examining educational selection presupposed dominant classes and a pyramidal division of labor. Strangely, Durkheim had studied these same pedagogic actions and emerged with a theory of education that was much more benign, much more socially unifying in its outcomes. Where Bourdieu and his associates saw conflict, Durkheim saw general consensus and mutual reinforcement of existing class structures and cultures.

Both Bourdieu and Durkheim saw that pedagogic action made children aware of what was and what was not important, worthwhile and necessary to learn. But they disagreed about whether such pedagogic actions were predominantly consensual or conflictual in nature and whether individuals were capable of influencing their schooling through reflection and action. Both agreed that those who were in harmony with the language and culture of the educational system had the best chance to do well in classrooms. Both saw this as a mechanism whereby the educational system maintained its structures and the culture it was required to reproduce. But Durkheim acknowledged that the lower classes often assimilated and accepted their status and possibilities in life, seeing small movements upward as significant gains in status and class.

Both of these men saw that children were included or excluded from the better schools because of their social origin and sex. Those who came from the more affluent families had better knowledge of the language and culture of the schools. Their diets were better, as were the schools they habitually attended. They usually had pedagogic experiences that validated their positions in the social and educational matrix of the nation. But Bourdieu believed that violence was done to the self-systems of youth from the lower classes and that this was done in the guise of open and fair competition, whereas Durkheim taught that schooling merely reinforced the cultural messages of the family.

A final comment: However unrelated these theories may be to the interaction individuals experience in classrooms, such efforts to understand and explain the persistent inequalities in schooling are desperately needed. If the ideas of Bourdieu and his associates seem too one-sided, too much couched in Marxist terms that ignore the individual, they nevertheless represent a serious attempt to study educational systems on a grand scale. Educational systems are conceived of as agencies that are connected to the social and economic life of societies, with constant reproductive functions and responsibilities. Nevertheless, a theory in which parents, teachers, and students are presented as robots who cannot understand or recognize the true nature of their work together seems to be too one-sided in its approach. These notions of powerless individuals living in depersonalized, bureaucratic societies seem accurate enough. But they reduce people to the role of players who are being moved by powerful unseen forces. That sociologists and social philosophers are moving away from the theories of cohesion that dominated in the 1950s may attest to the conflictual period which the world has lived through during the past forty years. It maybe that Bourdieu was right to see schooling as the center of inculcation in modern society, replacing the family and the church.

Certainly schooling's bureaucratic, administrative rationality attempts to control more and more of the thoughts and bodily movements of teachers and students. But in this, they are merely continuing practices linked to penal and mental institutions of the precapitalist period. It may be also that the theory of symbolic violence is describing pedagogic work better than more benign theories in our age of mass immigrations and increasing cultures of poverty. But as long as individuals' explanations of classroom life contradict those of theorists, scholars will have to look for supplemental theories or new methods of proving that misrecognition is in fact taking place in classrooms. Until then, the person who acts and understands will have to remain a part of social theory, even if his knowledge of the world is distorted by cultural and linguistic understandings and usage. Yes, the individual's perceptions suffer when he tries to transform the object world into an intelligible entity. When that world enters his stream of consciousness, it is changed significantly. Ideological assumptions come into play because the individual seldom understands that reality cannot be transformed into language and still remain reality. In fact, language categories often shape the very ways in which people can think about their environment and social relations. There is reason to assume that misrecogition is a normal human condition and that ideological thinking fulfills a human need to understand that which may be beyond understanding, namely, why are we here? What is the meaning of our lives? Finally, that which is unseen by the actors is often extremely important in structuring their experiences and interactions. Individuals often cannot see the internal relatedness between schooling and other features of the larger social formation. Perhaps we cannot reach a point at which grand theory can be used for operational research. But such formulations as the ones in this chapter provide us with a profound glimpse of schooling's functions and practices in an impersonal and increasingly secular world.

Sociocultural theorists will have to pay more attention to theses that provide logical propositions and glosses and search for hidden power relations beneath the surface of social amity and solidarity. The important problems for schooling in the twenty-first century will certainly revolve around problems of inequality and symbolic violence as they are played out for children in urban centers and in the emerging Third World. This focus will force us to face the effects of arbitrary cultural and linguistic habituses on the success or failure of children from different social origins and sexes.

4

Ideological State Apparatuses

After World War II, French intellectuals developed a structuralist tradition of thought that opposed humanist and empirical ideas of knowledge and history. Humanism had been dominant for centuries, basing itself on the creative abilities and genius of human beings; man was capable of knowing and subjugating nature and his social environment. He was the subject who acted, transforming the world, molding it closer to his needs and desires. Empiricism had allowed the physical sciences to make great progress in the nineteenth and twentieth centuries. Its successes caused the social sciences to imitate its methods, unsuccessfully. Empiricists believed there was no higher basis for knowledge than the experiences of individuals. The foundation for an understanding of social phenomena could only be lived experiences of people interacting in institutional settings. There was an unexplained but real coherence between the physical and social world and the individual's ability to grasp and articulate that world.

In the new structuralist perspectives, however, the individual was no longer seen as the source and certifier of meaning and consciousness. Now, he was a subject who was imprisoned in a world of consciousness dominated by language and linguistic categories. The structural linguistics of Saussure and Jakobson were the way these sociolinguists viewed the relationship between meaning and subjectivity.[1] In these theories, the linguistic sign was divided into two parts, that of the signifier and that of the signified. The sign or sound that signified an object or idea to another person was now seen as an arbitrary invention having little or no relation to that object or idea. The word described the object because of a convention that was agreed upon and understood by both parties to the communication. It did not identify the object under discussion in any other way. Thus the identity of an object such as a chair, to name one example, was not given by the object itself nor by the subject who used the word. The chair's identity was transmitted through a system of similarities and dissimilarities embedded in the structure of the language being spoken. The individual speaker was no longer seen as the subject who endowed the chair with the meanings we associate with the word.

Structural linguists also made an important distinction between language and speech. Any spoken word can send a message to a receiving other only if it does so within the rules and signs that are part of the language being used. The meaning of a statement, then, is never an expression of the inner reality of the speaker. On the contrary, the speaker must use discipline so that the language used is in conformance with the demands of a structured, impositional sign-system.

Structural linguists also studied entire language systems, giving priority to langue over parole. *Langue* can be loosely translated as linguistic system, conveying a sense of the grammatical structures supporting any spoken language. *Parole* deals with language behavior or what is actually said in ongoing interactions. Its focus is upon the actual spoken words between subjects in social situations. This focus away from the spoken word has important consequences. The structure of a linguistic system in its entirety determines the position of every other part of it, including the actually spoken words of individuals. Changing the meaning of one segment of a communication changes the meaning of every other feature of the signification system. The totality has priority in structuralist thought here and in its other applications in the behavioral sciences.

Second, the structure of language systems was not to be sought at an empirical level of understanding. The investigator had to follow the lead of psychoanalytic theory, searching for what lay behind and beneath linguistic structures and messages. What is seen by teachers and students in classrooms, as one example, is not the structure of their communication systems, but its effects, that is, the product of those structures. The structure of an individual's language is unconscious and not readily visible to the untrained observer. Yet the teacher or student can apply its grammatical and phonological rules without thinking about it. The ability to use linguistic constructions is a common genetic heritage that human beings of all stations in life possess. The number of languages spoken is limited yet incredibly diverse. But certain unchanging features consistently reappear in all of them.

A final point: this approach to the study of language is ahistorical and static, with little attention being paid to the changes occurring over time. The structures are the givens of every situation, universally present since the first communications between humans. In spite of the obvious modifications of language in the past, language systems have a timeless quality. Of course this approach isolates language from its social, economic, and historical contexts, from the praxis within which all language is formed and refined. Structural linguists seek to go beyond such analyses, searching for the laws that govern all language systems. There is much more to structuralism than these few ideas, of course. In fact, the concept covers such a wide variety of thought that it must be thought of as an umbrella term. Here we refer to it only as a precursor to Althusser's construction of structural Marxism.[2]

The anthropologist Lévi-Strauss used Saussure's ideas about sign and signification to explain the social practices of kinship, economic relations, food, and myth.[3] They were seen as communications that were also constructed within the rules of language. Lévi-Strauss's work described and analyzed them, showing their unity within particular cultures. Each was shown to be related to and derived from one another. By paying close attention to the structures behind these significations, he believed a universal language of the mind could be uncovered. The individual, a gain, was seen as a subject whose consciousness was illusory. Beyond language or signification codes, the individual had no ready access to social reality or intercourse. His cognition was language bound and further distorted by ideology and limited horizons. Lévi-Strauss saw in myths the social cement and cohesiveness of societies, whereby individuals were bound together by their common adherence to the signs and linguistic representations of their common social heritages.

The search for structuralist interpretations opposed to the subject-centered ideas of humanism and empiricism permeated depth psychology, too. Jacques Lacan developed a theory of the human psyche that used Marxism and psychoanalysis to de-center the individual in modern society.[4] Lacan used the concepts and ideas of structural linguistics to show that human consciousness was not possible without the intermediary instrument of language, that its own means of making sense out of the world depended upon linguistic categories and structures. Both the conscious and the unconscious thoughts of an individual were structured by language and signification codes. The phases through which the individual acquired his personal identity were analyzed through the categories of structural linguistics as stages in his submission to the rules and authority of the symbolic order, or culture.

Of course there were problems trying to relate the individualistic ideas of psychoanalysis to those of Marxism and social philosophy. Psychoanalysis seemed to have little or no use for the class analysis that was at the center of Marxian thought. Instead, it focused on the individual and his conflicts with himself and those around him. History seemed to be less relevant, even though Freud did do some interesting studies of important historical and biblical figures. Such ideas as the Oedipus complex were presented as universal truths that held true in every culture and at all times in human history. Psychoanalysis seemed to be able to interpret history as it was presented, but it did not seem interested in or capable of understanding the class structures that supported such representations. Although Freud did use historical data in his work with patients, delving into their social relations with relatives and friends, he related them only to the individual patient's problems. The neglect of historical specificity is characteristic of all schools of psychoanalytic thought and one of the central areas of critical concern.

IDENTITY AND THE SYMBOLIC ORDER

Returning to the ideas of Lacan, the actual subject of social interaction is not the unique, centered "ego" as portrayed by Freud or as he perceives himself to be in everyday encounters with others.[5] His sense of himself, his "center," is illusory, a misrecognition of the linguistic and ideological categories that he uses to recognize himself. Lacanian theory, rooted in materialistic suppositions of language and culture, reformulated the cogito of classical philosophy. That formulation presumed an individual who was a subjective agent experiencing the world around him. "I think, therefore I am," was the famous quotation. But now, that insight was turned on its head because of Freud's discoveries about the unconscious. The new statement, based on the de-centering of the individual, stated, "I think where I am not, and I am where I do not think."[6]

For Lacan, the genesis of human personality is divided into two structural concepts. These are the imaginary and the symbolic, and they are both genetic and structural in essence. The genetic refers to the evolution of the human child into masculine and feminine categories. This follows the development of the fetus and neonate to the end of the Oedipal period, when the animal is finally transformed into a small human child. This is the path that human beings follow in the development of their self-insights and social identities: from nature to culture in two significant steps. The first stage, labeled the mirror stage, describes the period in a child's life when he is concerned with only one other significant person, the mother or nurturing other. The neonate lives in dual intercourse, in a mode of imaginary fascination with the ego. He is at one and the same time himself and the other person, and any other person he comes in contact with. He is unable to take up the objectivity and understanding of the other or himself. This stage of development is ended when the infant enters the Oedipal period. A new structure emerges against the background of the fundamental relationship the child has formed with his mother. This new structure is intrusive and effects and transforms the imaginary satisfaction of both the child and his mother. It introduces the child to the symbolic order, the order of language categories, the objectifying order that allows him to say: "I am a boy. You are my mother. He is my friend. It is not important." The child can now situate himself as a human being in a world of adults and others that existed before he was born. He develops language to a point where he is able to take his place in the symbolic order. He is able to see himself as a member of a family, and he sees others outside that family. But these insights are confounded by the order of language, which limits and categorizes everything he sees, hears, and understands. In the Oedipal stage, he is reborn as a user and object of language. Now he is a designated person who is assigned to a family with a particular identity and class position in society. His existence becomes localized within the structures and laws of language, which establish and present him with his human role, with the human order he must now live in. For Lacan, these two stages of infancy contain the basic features for all future and imaginary situations the child will encounter in his life. They are the structural givens of all social intercourse and reality he will experience, perceive, and understand. The imaginary structures are those that take the "ego" to be the "I," the unified phenomenon, or the origin of all sensing and responding in the object world. The subject sees himself as the primary source of meanings without seeing also that he stands outside an articulation system that has defined him and the things he sees, hears, and understands. The idea of the ego as the center of human personality is changed into a linguistic construct without any real center. Individuals think, but they do so in the words, symbols, and ideas of others who have lived before them. It is this world of words that creates and sustains the world of objects. The attitudes and language of parents form an infant's first basis for understanding himself.[7] These symbols and cultural formations create an identity that the child then misrecognizes as his own. In this view of the social order, all practices can be understood by tracing them to previous understandings and exchanges; all social reality can be understood as an elaboration of language systems. Because social interaction is carried out through the dimension of language, it becomes necessary for scholars to study the ways in which language constructs the social and individual worlds of schools and work. In these social settings, the word becomes paramount, and the individual a linguistic and cultural construct. Language is an alien and alienating system of accounting, separated and apart from the reference world it is supposed to describe. It is the structure and order of language that, according to Lacan, completely conditions the individual's perceptions and comprehension of the object world.

SOME PROBLEMS

For Lacan, individuals suffer from a basic misunderstanding of language and the way it is used in the commonsense world. The subject, who is the source and response agent of successful usages at home and in schools, is ignored or thought of as an individual who is caught up in the process of the moment. The meaning of his communications are seldom related to past meanings, persons, or places. The subjects are viewed as actors who are seeking to bring the signifying chain to an end. Lacanian theory is concerned with placing the subject in his position within the language and social identity structure, with de-centering the individual by showing the linguistic constructs that are the focus of misperceptions and misunderstandings.[8]

According to Lacan, the person is constructed in language and linguistic symbols and has no other real center beyond the social one he has learned to misrecognize as himself. An understanding of the human psyche, social history, and the social and economic laws of society are now to be sought in the study of language. All intercourse is to be seen as understandings, as streams of linguistic consciousness, as significations that systematically decipher and transform the object world. Social reality is now a linguistic phenomenon, the place in which the person is constructed and reconstructed.

The disappearance of the individual in Marxist thought is not a new development. Lacan's work traces the development of the neonate but does not give sufficient consideration to prenatal and preverbal experiences. These primary psychic energies predominate at the beginning of an individual's life. They are not rooted in language. Rather they are preverbal, genetic structures that provide the first glimpses of consciousness for the neonate, and possibly for the prenatal fetus as well. A fundamental theory of psychoanalysis can provide us with the limitations of Lacan's theories. The theory of psychic determinism, as Freud conceived it, states that all mental life is determined by previous emotions and experiences. In the life of the mind, nothing is left to chance or random selection. Each psychic occurrence is predetermined and related to others that preceded it in time and that influence how events are processed and understood in the present. Mental events may seem unrelated to the individual as he lives out his daily life, but this is only his misapperception of reality. Beneath the surface, mental life is no more able to operate without causal connections to previous events than are physical phenomena. Discontinuity does not exist in the life of the mind. This fact would indicate that the formative periods when the self is created occurs without language and without a fully formed psyche. The thoughts and emotions of the prenatal and neonatal periods are concerned with bodily needs and functions. Lacan is right when he traces the development from nature to culture, from primary thinking to secondary verbal communication. But he ignores the preverbal experience of the newborn child. It is there, according to Kris, Spitz, Hartmann, and Mahler, that the personality of an individual is formed.[9,10] The ego develops from an undifferentiated mental apparatus, because it is genetically predisposed to do so. This is when the neonate and infant first learn to respond to the world of language and culture.

A second important psychoanalytic theory may now be introduced to show some further difficulties with Lacan's formulations. The theory of consciousness indicates that conscious behavior is comparatively rare in human beings. The unconscious plays a dominating role in the mental life of the individual, confounding even his understanding of language as it is ordinarily used in everyday life. Lacan's theories are too rigid, too fascinated with rational structures and insights. Freud and Heinz Hartmann, two giants in the field of psychoanalysis, believed that the constructs of the ego, the id, and the superego were ideal types that could help us to better understand the workings of the mind. But they also stated that such structures were to be understood in a dynamic way. The actual processes of thought and emotion were intertwined and impossible to separate in actuality. All of human personality had conscious, preconscious, and unconscious features, which were in perpetual movement and conflict. The center of the individual was determined in the preverbal period of his life and influenced how he interpreted everything that came afterward, including linguistic facility. Lacan's work is valuable because it points to that which can be studied rationally, that which is crucial in social intercourse between persons. But his conclusions are overdrawn because he does not give sufficient consideration to the preverbal, irrational, primary energies and images of the neonate.

Even language, which is at the center of Lacan's work, has a different, symbolic meaning in the mental life of individuals. In dreams, in unconscious life, words often have many meanings or take on meanings which are nonrational and largely symbolic representations of past experiences. It is this secret language of symbols and repressed emotions that is both the core and the mystery of the individual's personality.

More obvious problems associated with any attempt to unite Marxism and psychoanalysis can no longer be avoided. There is a profound conflict between these disciplines, both of which have revolutionized the way we think about ourselves and society. Psychoanalysis speaks of human consciousness in which the individual is unaware of and not in control of his impulsive life. His power to control his behavior is often uncertain, at best. Marx, on the other hand, described and analyzed history in terms of classes struggling for supremacy at different times in human history. Consciousness, when mentioned at all, was framed in the language of political awareness and objective needs. Class interests and political goals were to be served by an awakening of subservient groups to their true position in society and in political action to change their conditions. Such demands for political action postulated, by implication, a subject who could think and feel and could develop higher levels of consciousness. The classes in modern society were seen by Marx as essential features of the relations between labor and capital, between those who controlled the means of production and those who were forced to sell their labor in the production processes. The accounts proposed by Lacan and Althusser are not in harmony with Marx's earlier theories. Class is hardly spoken of in these new linguistic constructions of social reality. An ahistorical structuralism predominates, with insights that are supposed to be valid for every society. They do provide an explanation of the importance of sexual identity in the labor market and society, thus filling a void in Marxian and Durkheimian sociology. They also provide insights into the families and schools as ideological state apparatuses responsible for the reproduction of educational and social relations of production. But the theories of Lacan and Althusser are couched in organic, structural categories of thought reminiscent of the nineteenth century. Placing so much emphasis on the effects of the first years of life places individuals under a burden that makes it difficult for them to control or change their relationships with others. It leaves men and women to struggle with their sexual identities even as it designates those identities as misrecognitions of linguistic and ideational constructs emanating from their earliest experiences.

Of course there are other ways to explain these phenomena, as Simmel showed more than a century ago. People are not just subject to the social institutions they live in; they are capable of struggling to change these mimetic structures, these givens, as recent events in Eastern Europe seem to indicate. The struggle between life and form presents us with a more dynamic theoretical construction.[11] Weber and Durkheim, among others, were aware of mimetic structures that appeared to individuals as immutable social formations. But such forms have changed over time, and the changes were begun by subjects who were acting on the object world in which they lived. Gintis and Bowles, whom we will discuss later in this book, have more recently demonstrated how the structural and relational features of schooling in the United States are related to the social relations of production. Schooling is seen as a social institution completely integrated into the labor market and economic system of society.

From this, we take the position that the individual cannot be seen as a person existing in a timeless and classless vacuum. The resolution of the Oedipal phase cannot be the final resolution of human personality, and the acquisition of social identity cannot be seen as a separate occurrence, apart from the larger social and economic life of the family's position in society. The effects of social-class stratification are pervasive. Within each family, traditional understandings help members cope with the past and face the present. Different attitudes toward schooling, the sexes, and the economic system, are all passed on in this primal process. But the family is always operating in history, as are the schools. Both are affected by their place in the economic and social structure of a particular social order. Both are physically located in ways that accentuate their positions in the social pyramid. Individuals learn of their class, ethnic, racial, and religious identities, but they do so imperfectly. Still, these identities, along with gender, play a decisive role in the experiences they have in school and the labor market. Sex differences affect the way that boys and girls are socialized and streamed in schools and universities. Class identities determine which schools a student attends and how well he or she will do there. Ethnic and racial identities will delimit the possibilities of life for many children, and religious affiliations also affect their life chances. Yet all of these children will develop an identity that includes but also transcends these linguistically transmitted structures learned since infancy. Their impulsive system will give to their personalities a distinctiveness and a subjectivity that should not be ignored or denied. These individuals will strive to achieve their perceived interests, no matter how much they seem to misrecognize those interests, no matter how much unconscious motivations determined their actions.

Of course families and schools should not be thought of as autonomous agencies. They are affected by the socioeconomic, by the relations they have to productive forces in society. These institutions are organizations that reproduce the labor power in society and are in turn reproduced by their own practices and the needs of the state that legitimates them. This does not mean that economics is the sole determinant of an individual's identity and experience, but it is surely one of the most important factors.

Continuing with the work of Lacan and Althusser, we offer this criticism: theories that see structural determinants such as signification codes and cultures as separate and apart from individuals, their class positions, and historical conditions have wandered far from Marx's and Freud's ideas and insights. Psychoanalysis is one discipline that understands what Lacan apparently does not. The structures of conscious life are determined by unconscious motivations, which are a part of the individual's psyche, his personality structure. Linguistic constructs are a part of this human identity equation, but only a part of it.

To repeat, the idea of linguistic and cultural determinants limits and constrains the action of individuals, ignoring the irrational and impulsive features of human personality. The structures of grammar and syntax do form parameters that limit the ways individuals can describe and understand their universe, as structuralists have shown. But they are also influenced by the personal, ongoing histories, by the socioeconomic hierarchy, and by the unconscious, impulsive features of human personality. The structures to which sociolinguists refer are not immutable, as they believe. They can be transformed by human beings who act to dissolve or change the relations they have with one another and with themselves.

All this is to say that a theory that reduces individuals to objects appears to be too static, unable to explain the social, economic, and emotional world. To make the individual a mere object means he or she can no longer struggle with the forms encountered in social life. Lacan and Althusser's theories shed light on the world of rational discourse governed by language and culture. But they cannot be accepted as a complete description of human reality, because the development of the individual's identity is more than just the linguistic, ideational impressions of others. Such theories are forced to ignore the irrational, impulsive, psychic energies that individuals use to locate and maintain themselves and their places in an increasingly alienated world.

IDEOLOGIES AND THE STATE CHANGE

It remained for Althusser to bring these ideas together in more cohesive fashion by developing a complex set of theories about ideology and ideological state apparatuses.[12] The functions of these state apparatuses were to be found in the reproduction of the conditions of production that prevailed in a given society, in the social relations of production Marx had made the center of his studies a century earlier. Althusser's central idea was that all ideological thought postulated individuals as subjects, empirically observable. These concrete persons were then subjected to the language, culture, and socializing processes of the family, the state, and religion, to name but a few of these state apparatuses. Ideology, in this theoretical formulation, represented the imaginary relations of individuals to their real conditions of existence, their relation to those conditions of social and economic life which structured their everyday existence.[13] For Althusser, ideology is ahistorical, omnipresent, and immutable in its forms. A series of apparatuses—the church, schools, family, political parties, trade unions, mass media—act as ideological conduits for the state.

These theories have an internal consistency that is compelling but lacks a sense of the historical, real world. That world is subordinated to abstract and rigid theoretical principles, and the everyday life of the individual becomes little more than a stream of consciousness carried along by linguistic transformations of worldly images. The ideological thoughts and learnings the individual imbibes from birth are not a reflection of the real state of affairs in his everyday life. His thought is contained in a parallel world, rather than in the world of social problems, practices, and conflicts. In this theoretical world, ideology is a form of social cohesion that unites societies and keeps them from coming apart. In this sense Althusser's work is in the tradition of Comte and Durkheim, two writers who tended to see social cohesiveness as the central problem and explanation for educational and social practices.

Althusser goes on to ask, within the theoretical framework of his theory of ideological state apparatuses, what one could reasonably expect from sociocultural theories of the schools.[14] He decides they should provide a conceptual framework that locates educational production within the socioeconomic and political formations of the particular society within which schools functioned. This means that educational systems and their practices would be related to the labor market and economic conditions prevailing in the surrounding culture. Such approaches would acknowledge that socioeconomic conditions play a commanding role in determining how schools are funded and operated in the modern world and how they perform their social functions of acculturation and social stratification. Althusser further believed that the conceptual and theoretical framework of sociocultural inquiries into schooling had to pay attention to and describe educational work and its outcomes in the most specific terms possible. To do so, they would have to rely upon the psychological and social science disciplines. These alone could help to explain how and why individuals act and react as they do once they are inside schools. They would also have need of sociolinguistics and ethnomethodological insights in order to learn more about the structure of language and the suppositions and accounting methods that often distort our understandings of social encounters. Two important points need emphasis: The use of insights and data from social science research will transform such data in the process because each discipline has within it substantive assumptions about the nature of social action and reality. Further, the disciplines have methodological assumptions about the appropriate methods for performing social science research. They often fail to deal with their assumptions of an orderly social world and the ways in which their coding methods distort what they are attempting to study.

IDENTITY AND THE EDUCATIONAL ORDER

The personality development of students in schools is a conflict-ridden rite of passage. Youngsters come to the classroom with a personal identity, a sense of themselves that involves illusion and misrecognition, as both Lacan and Althusser would describe their preschool relations. These are based on a misrecognition of the linguistic and ideological constructs that parents have used to describe them as their individual identities, their inner cores. Nevertheless, it is this personal front or identity that students recognize as their own in the empirical world. Before they enter their first classroom, they have suppositions about themselves and the school they are to attend. Once they enter into the interaction itself, they make adjustments to the new realities that present themselves. That the individual appears to think in classroom situations is beyond challenge. But most of his or her thinking seems to take place before or after the fact, as Lacan noted in his rewriting of Descartes' cogito. While in the classroom, the student seems to react as if in a dream, without thinking or questioning the demands of the teacher. Silence rules and regimentation are accepted with little thought. It is only afterward that these schoolroom encounters are transformed into language and ideas, only then that the student develops conscious attitudes toward them. He or she hates this teacher or likes that one, doesn't understand arithmetic but is interested in history, and so on.

We may say that the child has two stages in the genesis of his organizational identity in schools. The first deals with the presenting front, which he presents to the school and which he possessed, more or less, before he began his schooling experiences. The second is his identity within the school building, which he will acquire through social interaction with teachers and other students. The first refers to the identity that the child was given in interaction with parents, family members, and neighborhood friends. The identity was usually more supportive and accepting, since it was formed by the language, culture, and ideas of kinsmen. They are what Ferdinand Tonnies referred to as Gemeinschaft relationships, in which the entire personality of the child was known to different members of his primary group. The personality formed in such circumstances was more intimate and encompassed all of the child's abilities and characteristics. But in the classroom experience, the child's gemeinschaft relationships are replaced by those of the contract or use relationship, that is, the Gesellschaft. Now he is transformed into a student and forced by state attendance laws to play the role the educational system has assigned to him. He is to be the ignorant person, no matter how well prepared he is when he enters the grade system. That is why he needs instruction; that is why he needs to be told what to do, when to do it, and so on. This, then, is the path the individual student follows in the further development of his social identity. He is defined by language once more, and by his ability to understand and master the arbitrary language and culture of the schools.

The first stage of a student's life in schools is characterized by a desire to recreate the gemeinschaft he had with his mother, to transfer feelings and attitudes to the new authority person, the teacher. The new student soon learns, however, that he lives in an insecure and confused environment. He is now quite clearly the other, the person who is the subject of the teachers monotonous impositions and demands. There is a lack of personal feeling, now. His understanding of himself and of others becomes more acute. His place in the educational system becomes more clear, and he begins to see himself and his social position in the classroom. This stage can be said to end when the child becomes aware of himself as a member of a distinct group and identifies with the ideas and language of that group. Masculinity and femininity gradually become more important.

His daily life becomes localized in classrooms, language interactions, and folklore, which establish and present him with his scholastic role, with the social order he must now live in for a good part of each day. These encounters in classrooms form the basis for much of the social identity that a youngster assumes in schools and society. The "I" now becomes enmeshed in the classroom identity, which it must assume in the organizational setting of the schools. The subject sees himself as the primary source of meanings but now sees and feels the educational system's structures, which have defined him anew and determined what he can and cannot learn. The idea of the ego, or the student's personal identity, is challenged by the definition of teachers and others.

Individuals think, but they think in words, symbols, and ideas that reflect the thoughts of significant others in their past. It is the world created by words and culture that sustains the classroom world for the child. It is the attitudes and language of the teacher that now form his basis for understanding himself, his competency and self-worth. It is the language and ideology of the schools that must now be mastered. In this school world, all practices can be understood by referring to previous ones, all goals can be seen as elaborations of previous goals and language that occurred in the past. But all the encounters cannot be reduced to language alone, even though language is the means through which schooling is achieved. There are the emotional and genetic features of the child's identity to be taken into account. Even though classroom interaction is carried out through the medium of language, this language cannot be understood unless it is related to the historical past and to the realities in the world of work that the schools are attempting to reproduce. The word is important, but the individual who must find his place in the social and economic structures of school and society has an identity above and beyond his misperceived, linguistic one. He has a gender identity, a race and class identity, an ethnic affinity, and so on. These also condition his perceptions of himself and the world within which he learns.

Some key questions can no longer be avoided. These have to do with schooling's reproductive functions and the ideology of schooling, which can confound students for many years. Then there are schooling's practices and traditions and the need of the economy to reproduce the human resources it needs as older workers retire and die and technology changes. Schooling is not a mirror of the workplace, by any means. Still, the apolitical and asocial analyses of the constitution of individuals and their interaction in schools misses the point completely. The father is not the boss, no matter how authoritarian he may seem at times. His authority is based on traditional and filial responsibilities and not on economic power to hire and fire. In a similar manner, the teacher is not the foreman, no matter how authoritarian and impositional his behavior may be in the classroom. Both of these figures play their part in preparing youth for the world of work, but they do so without ever being aware of what they are actually doing. As the child matures, he may learn more about politics and science, he may come to despise the beliefs and values of his parents for a while. He may even succeed in school, transcending his social status and entering a high-status occupation. In most instances, he becomes more aware of sex and race, more aware of the consequences these have for his own life. But the individual's family has its own history and its own relations with others in society. And these histories and present conditions come together to determine the kind of neighborhood school a child will attend and the possibilities he will have to go on to college and a better-paying job or profession. Members of families acquire social class identities that they share with one another. These are influenced by sexual differences, which further determine the kind of schooling and work and individual will or will not receive. These two dimensions, the sexual and the socioeconomic, come together to limit further the success and mobility of individuals when they enter the schools or the labor market. The family, the schools, and the state are social structures that are part of a larger design, one which has its roots in economics but is not limited to economics alone. Schools and families are state apparatuses that mirror institutions in the economic and political world they live in. They are not semiautonomous or autonomous social formations divorced from the class structure of society. The family and schools need to be seen as outgrowths of the social relations that have developed in a particular society. What is more, they are a fundamental part of the process by which the society and economy replenish themselves from generation to generation. The struggle to succeed in schools reflects the general desire of the poor and laboring classes to lift themselves out of their current status into higher socioeconomic levels.

In summary, the individual–object dialectic has dominated western thought since Descartes. In it, the Cartesian ego creates the social world and reconstitutes it into language and knowledge, thus affirming its own existence. For Lacan and Althusser in the post-Freudian, post-Einsteinian era, this subject who sees, hears, senses, and understands his environment is now an object. As object, his identity, sight, hearing, speech, and senses are all formed in social and educational production. They are an outgrowth of ideology and the language and ideas that the individual learned as an infant to recognize as himself. The ego's knowledge is thus problematic, at best. The people in schools and at work are subject to it and can do little more than react to the givens they encounter in different classrooms. They participate in a world that was made before them and speak a language taught to them by others who lived in the past.

Since Althusser and Lacan have transformed the individual in humanist discourse into an individual who is now an object, some questions seem in order: Are teachers and students capable of knowing and understanding the classroom world in which they live and work? Do they have the means for knowing external objects and situations there? And if they do, how is this done in everyday situations?

Two possibilities present themselves: First, the knowing teacher or student has some mechanism for gaining direct access to what is going on around her. But this possibility has been undermined by the work of Lacan and Althusser. It assumes that the classroom world exists in knowable forms and that the knowing teacher or student has the cognitive abilities to recognize and understand what is happening.

A second way suggests that knowledge of classroom life can be achieved only through the means of signification systems and language, which is the path Althusser and Lacan have chosen. Yet problems persist. How can we know for certain that there is a correlation between the classroom's reality and the person's ability to perceive that reality? How can we know that a correlation exists between the subject and the object in the classroom situation? As no direct access to the real world of the classroom can be accepted here, the process involves a transformation from reality to language and consciousness. For empiricists, observation and the gathering of data are the ways in which different theories of social and school life can be validated. Rationalists seek internal consistency in their thought and concepts, using them to assure the relationship between the knowing teacher or student and the school world that needs to be apprehended.

Althusser focused much of his critique on rationalist perspectives, believing others had discredited empiricism. His own structuralist theories were an example of rationalism. As they were also grounded in Marxism, however, he treated them as privileged. They were the beginning and cause of problematics and a method of solving problems within the historical materialism of Marxist theory. Validation, in Althusser's sense, came only by referring concepts to the basic ideas of Marxism. This arbitrary closure of discourse, almost theological in nature, harkened back to notions that Marxism was a science separate and apart from the other social sciences.

A problem with these rationalist perspectives comes readily to mind: If the world is not rational, much that falls outside such thought must be omitted. The ideas of the teacher or student now determine what is and is not real or significant. They determine how the relations between various structural and relational features of classroom life will be internally related to one another. Logic, with its emphasis on inclusion and exclusion concepts comes to determine what can and cannot be thought of as real (and significant). Thought is given a preeminent place in the teacher's or student's perception of classroom reality. The real world is effectively transformed into an individual teacher's or student's stream of consciousness. This presupposes that classroom life and the individual teacher's or student's stream of consciousness are separate and not internally related in any way.

This work of creating the social self takes place in the family, at first, and seems to conform to the work of Schutz.[15] Individuals are constituted in the family. Through language they learn who they are and how they must regard themselves in their relations with others. They are not the center of their own experiences, even though they experience individual encounters as though happening to them alone. From Freud and his followers, we have learned of the contradictory, confused, unconscious, and many-sided nature of human personality. This idea contrasts sharply with the ideal of the controlled and controlling individual of the humanist period. The entrance into language, communication, and complicated social relationships occurs over a long period of time. The identity of the subject is formed and reformed into an imaginary identity, which is both personal and social in nature. He comes to see himself as others see him and to accept their images as his essential core. He comes to recognize himself, or as Lacan puts it, to misrecognize these linguistic and ideational constructs as his inner self, because these identifications of the self are language bound and idealized and show him to be an active doer and shaper of his environment. This misrecognition of the nature of the self forms the core of ideological thought, consciousness, action, and experience both for individuals and for social institutions such as the family and educational systems.

The problems students have in schools are compounded by the ideology of schooling. Even though educators pay homage to democracy and human equality, their pedagogical practices are opposed to these ideas. Teachers want not freedom for their students but dominance and control. They have no taste for individualism and intellectual curiosity but rather demand that youngsters accept regimentation and control as their daily fare. Teachers need conformity and obedience even as they talk about competition and the rights of the individual. In order to prepare students for the workplace and to maintain their own organizational structures and power, teachers (and school administrators) need a state that can assure them a monopoly of the means of educational production in society. In this way they are able to secure the reproduction of the educational and economic system from one decade to the next. Teachers (and school administrators) require a powerful state that can formulate policies that assure a maintenance of the status quo. Schooling, finally, needs a state that will keep the competing needs of different classes in check and assure a curriculum and educational culture steeped in ideological understandings of the state and the economy. Whereas reformers sometimes seek to end the stratified knowledge and tracking systems now in place, teachers (and school administrators) demand a return to high standards and basics. Where reformers sometimes speak of integration and an end to testing, school authorities pay lip service to these ideas but continue to function in the old ways. Where reformers speak of broadening the educational opportunities of all children, educational authorities point to the failure of the poorer classes to achieve even when they were given preferential treatment, that is, the educational preparation and knowledge all students are supposed to receive in state-supported schools.

The demand for a policy of accountability affects the entire culture of the competition-bound, stratified educational system. The teachers (and school administrators) cease to be benign figures who are trying to help children to prepare for adulthood. Horace Mann and the original proponents of common, state-supported schools believed in a common education for all, but they were soon forced to change their minds. State-supported public education has long since abandoned such ideas in the face of persistent poverty and the failure of schools to teach the children of the poor successfully.

The modern educational system had its origins in the needs of states to bind their people in bonds of national union, in inculcation. These impulses found their natural outlet in the common schools, because these structures encouraged students to accept economic and social structures as timeless entities that could never be changed. As an ideal there is still talk of a common education for all, a striving to unite the people of a nation into one patriotic unit. But competition holds sway in the capitalist nations, and with each new generation educational systems set limits and barriers that cannot be overcome by most children in the working and lower middle classes. This competition in schools is an economic necessity, as any movement to break down the class structure creates conflict and reduces the system's ability to reproduce and maintain itself. Grounded in needs of the state and the economy, schooling is ideologically justified by reference to the defense and occupational needs of the nation. There is less and less talk of democratic beliefs in equity for all classes, races, and minorities. Rather, the economic advantage of the few is seen in the private schools they attend and in the stratification of institutions of higher education. As the schools form a status pyramid, private schools and universities are at the top, catering to those who will assume positions of power and leadership in their adulthood. Thus, in educational ideology as in the political sector of society, there emerges a democratically cloaked power foundation that is really dedicated to keeping the lower classes in their place, both educationally and in the economic arena. In place of the democratic values of equal access to knowledge and power, a plutocratic ideal of dominance and mastery appears and makes itself felt in the schoolroom practices students experience every day. This mastery of the student is done in the name of the business and professional classes against the interests of unions and workers.

More recently the ideology of the nation-state has come into vogue in Europe and the United States. It glorifies the nation-state even as it talks about European union and the United Nations, and these ideas are passed on to children in neighborhood schools. What an illusion it is to preach goodwill and cooperative endeavors in an educational system and world where competition and conflict decide everything, where the strong dominate the weak everywhere on the globe. What foolishness to look forward to more humane schools and societies when only force and power act as arbiters of differences between nations and classes. What an illusion to try to legislate integration and equality in schools that have been committed to racial separation and stratification of the classes for so many years. What right have reformers to demand preferential treatment for the poorer and minority populations in schools and workplaces? Are they unaware of the internal-relatedness of discrimination and the economic and social conditions in their countries? Could schools ever be called upon to teach their students to be discontented with their educational, economic, and social destinies? To ask such questions seems foolish indeed.

In place of the ideals of democracy, schooling offers only endless competition and failure for millions of youngsters. Schools are able to understand the conflicts that often arise between the haves and the have-nots. But they cannot offer them a better, more promising future. Their physical and organizational structures are steeped in authoritarianism, with roots extending backward into the precapitalist period of history. The construction of the modern individual in mass society takes place in these ideological state institutions, where the selves of students are molded to suit the needs and demands of a pyramidal school system and economy.

Finally, some key questions remain: Any attempt to define the idea of modes of production must make a distinction between labor and labor power, both in school and in the economic arena. Labor power refers to that which is produced in the families and schools under more personal and sheltered circumstances than one finds in the economic sector of society. The relations between capital and labor are quite different from those of parents and children or teachers and students, as was noted earlier. In both processes raw materials are transformed in a labor process that makes it an economic phenomenon, reproducing the labor power that will be needed in the future. Yet the domestic labor of the family or the work of schoolteachers does not seem to reckon with profit and loss as one finds in the economic arena. The existence of mothers and fathers, of teachers, indicates that the time needed to produce labor power cannot be calculated in terms of dollars per hour or in terms of adequate wages. The idea of exploitation also seems less applicable, as any surplus value created by the labor of parents and teachers is in the distant future and does not conspicuously enter into the relationships. The time spent by mothers shopping, cooking, reading to their children, and so on is rewarded in ways that ignore such items as labor time and wages. These parental duties are performed even when the woman of the house also holds down a full-time job outside the home. Likewise, the time spent by schoolteachers in their classrooms is also rewarded in ways that ignore ideas about labor time and wages, and teachers continue to be underpaid and neglected by those politicians and businessmen who are outside the schools. Domestic labor and labor in the sheltered professions cannot be understood in terms of the normal processes of commodity production. Neither the family nor the schools can be seen as agencies that exploit one another in order for surplus labor to be appropriated by one of them. Noneconomic coercion propels men and women to labor in their homes and to support those homes, and children to attend state schools and help in the running of those homes. Noneconomic supports also fuel the relations between teachers and students, even though much of their work together in classrooms mimics the social relations of the workplace.[16]

We may conclude with the following: Domestic and educational labor are not commodity-producing labor, even though they result in reproducing the labor power of such labor. They may be said to transform the individual child, but that transformation is qualitatively different from commodity production, which changes raw materials into consumable forms and goods. The transformation of the individual child does produce values and ideas that allow for the maintenance of the economic conditions in society. But the relationships between boss and workers, between capitalists and laborers seems to be different from those of families and schools. Both of these state ideological apparatuses can be seen as preindustrial forms of socialization and production that continue to contribute to modern-day methods of economic and social production. Both have roots in tradition, and the relations between individuals are governed by social scripts and ideologies that differ from those seen in the workplace.

5

The Social Relations of Production

Until now we have talked about production in capitalist society without explaining what we mean. According to Marx, the process of making commodities is one way that unpaid surplus labor is extracted from workers and used by capitalists for their own advantage.[1] Workers and capitalists come together in an unequal relationship, which determines who rules and is ruled in the workplace. Owners of the means of production set the conditions under which labor will be performed. The free worker, in this process, is in reality a "hireling." The only force that brings owners and workers together is their common pursuit of money and personal interest. The producer is unconcerned about individuals he employs save as they satisfy his need to create surplus value from their labor. Labor is viewed as a commodity, a cost of doing business. The free laborer becomes a worker only when capital is available to make use of him. In Marx's words, the worker can "exist as capital only as long as capital exists to use him.[2] The existence of capital is his existence; it shapes the content of his life, though remaining indifferent to it. The workman who is subject to this fate can hardly be anything else but a commodity in human form, an individual not belonging to himself but alienated from himself."[3] The "free" worker is free in theory only. In reality, he does not control the forces upon which his existence depends. The work he needs to sustain himself and his family is given to him by capital, and this work can be denied him. The wages paid, the ways in which work is accomplished, the location and conditions under which workers are rewarded or dismissed, all influence the manner in which people relate to one another in their social lives. For Marx, writing more than a century ago, the crucial element in the production process was

precisely these social relations that developed between those who owned the instruments of production and those who were compelled to sell
their labor power to these owners.

In *Capital,* Marx used the concept of surplus value to define specific
economic forms of exploitation in capitalist society. Surplus value referred to the difference between goods produced and goods consumed by
the work force. In the process, the surplus value created by workers was
expropriated by capitalists. The exploitation increased with rising rates
of productivity because the worker was able to produce more surplus
value, which owners then disposed of as they wished. The worker became
poorer as he produced more in modern factories, as his productivity increased. With new technology, he became less valuable to capitalists who
constantly sought cheaper sources of labor. In this way, labor "produces
not only commodities: it produces itself and the worker as a commodity—
and does so" in ways that dehumanize the worker and his employer.

In order to understand how surplus value is generated in the production process, it is necessary to analyze labor power as a cost of doing
business, as a commodity.[4] Of course labor is not a commodity in any
ordinary sense of the word. But workers' efforts are figured in when the
costs of production are estimated by employers. They are just one more
resource that needs to be put in place. The worker performs services at
the bidding of his employer, presenting himself at the location and time
chosen by others. The employer uses capital to buy the labor power of
the employee, directing him to complete tasks as he is presented with
them. The use of the workers' brains and muscle power are not discussed at this stage of the hiring process, although employers often include
these in their initial calculations of cost. Only when employees actually
do the work can their thinking ability or strength come into play. A re-
ceptionist can or cannot think well on her feet. A steelworker can or cannot perform the physical tasks of his work. The power to use labor is inherent in the employers' ability to pay wages for the workers' time and
energies.

Labor power in capitalist society is a commodity because it has a value
similar to other commodities. It is bought and sold at the going market
prices. Marx wrote that the value of labor power is determined by the
amount of labor time needed for production and reproduction of a special
article.[5] In the case of labor power, it is the amount of time needed to
maintain and reproduce his labor power from one day to the next. An
employee needs maintenance, much as machinery does. He or she must
have food, clothing, housing, and so on, and these needs must be met
if the worker is to continue working. Of course these needs are culturally and historically determined and vary from civilization to civilization.
The value of labor power can be given as a quantifiable cost similar to
the costs of other needed commodities.

Surplus value, then, is a consequence of the production process. But how does it occur? The capitalist decides on a business venture and decides to purchase machinery, materials, and labor power in order to produce the commodities he thinks will make him a profit. He then combines these into a production process that causes new commodities to be made and sent into the marketplace. But the aim of the capitalist is to increase the amount of capital he has, and when the productive process is completed and the goods sold, he usually does have more money than he began with. Where did he get this surplus value?

Marx showed that surplus value could not come about by simply buying and selling commodities themselves.[6] If those who sold raw materials and machinery gained a profit of 10 percent, and those who sold their manufactured commodities did the same, no one would benefit. The former would lose when he sought to buy manufactured commodities, and the latter when he bought the materials he needed to continue producing goods. The materials themselves could not account for the surplus value because their value at the beginning of the production process was there at the end, but there was no reason to assume their value had increased. A diamond set in a ring does not increase its value, even though the ring itself may very well do so. Marx also showed that the same is true of machinery and materials. Neither of them can transfer to the finished commodity any more value than they themselves contain. It is the workmanship that changes the diamond ring into something more valuable than it was before it became an object of productive labor. But how is this accomplished?

The capitalist uses his resources to purchase labor power at the going rate; he pays the worker wages that will allow him to subsist. Marx used the following example: The value of labor power equals the amount of work that can be accomplished in six hours. That is the amount needed for one worker to sustain himself (and his family). After an employee has worked for six hours, he "has added to the value of the materials and machinery used up—a value which we know reappears in the product—an additional value sufficient to cover his own means of subsistence." If the worker were to stop working at this point, the capitalist would be able to sell his merchandise and "reimburse himself for his outlays." There would be no profit. There would be no growth of capital. But the worker has sold his labor power to the employer for a day, and most working days are longer than six hours. The worker continues to add value to the products he produces, but now this value is above and beyond what is needed to meet his own subsistence needs. This value is pocketed by the capitalist, who sees it as his reward for having the initiative to organize, finance, manage, and retail commodities. Marx goes on to show that the capitalist paid for each commodity in the production process, including the labor power needed to transform the cotton, spindle, and so forth into yarn. His price reflects the demands of the market, yet his profit comes from the surplus value created by the worker's efforts beyond the time needed for his own subsistence. The worker's laboring day is thus divided by Marx into two parts, needed labor and surplus labor. Of course necessary labor and surplus labor appear in all societies that are above the primitive level. In slave states of the American south, the labor of the slave was expropriated by the plantation-owning class, who maintained their control over slaves by denying them wages for the labor they performed. Slavers purchased the slave, not his or her labor power. It was understood that the slave was a piece of property and would do whatever work owners gave them to do. The force of law assured that these conditions of labor would be adhered to by both parties, with runaway slaves being severely punished when they were recaptured. In the factories and offices of capitalist enterprises, however, the relationship between employees and employers is a use one, often supported by legal definitions of responsibilities and contracts. Nevertheless, the worker, like the slave, is selling his labor power. The difference is that this is done for eight hours a day or for clearly stipulated periods of time. Still, both sell their labor power. One works to survive or subsist, the other to receive wages that will allow him and his family to do the same. What is special about exploitation in capitalist society is not its existence but the form it takes, that is, the production of surplus value that capitalists use for their own purposes.

Exploitation in capitalist systems can be measured by the surplus value a worker produces in the workplace; it is capitalism's raison d'être. Commodities must be transformed into profits, that is, into further capital. This requirement forces a differentiation between the labor a worker performs to meet his subsistence needs and the work he does beyond this level of productivity. When the capitalist markets his goods a further differentiation comes into play: effective demand and demand that must go unheeded. Effective demand exists only where the individual has the money needed to acquire the desired commodity.

The essence of the commodity is the separation of a thing's use value from its exchange value. Yet the commodity should not be thought of as an economic category only. The commodity concept makes the possession of things man's strongest link to the physical world. It divides people into buyers and sellers, centering economic activity on the production and distribution of commodities. The effect is that everything, including natural phenomena and human personality, become meaningful only in their commercial aspects. The tendency to value commodities or things carries with it an inclination to devalue anything that cannot be reduced to a commodity. Thus material values have become predominant in modern times.

These insights into the production of material wealth allow Marx to place the exploitation inherent in class relations on an objective basis instead of using moralistic or subjective ideas about ethics and equity. They are central to Marx's theories of history and his ideas about the totality of social relations. Relations that develop in the production process are social ones, signifying where a society is in its historical development. Economic relations can be seen as social ones that designate a specific historical period. They are included within the relations developing in the production process and so have a deep and lasting influence on all forms of social intercourse. Capital has a need to expand, often beyond the process of production. In the distribution of goods, there is a need for ever higher levels of profits. This effects the distribution and circulation problems associated with getting commodities to market. It also affects consumption patterns and is in turn affected by such patterns. The forms of domination in capitalist society and the limits of such domination can be concretely observed in the production processes. Domination extends only to the workplace; in his personal life, the worker is "free." Marx was specific in his belief that the concrete, historical development of these forms of social relations was more important than any philosophical concepts that could be postulated from them. His work sought to create a theory that was, in contrast to Althusser's work, deeply tied to the real world. He did not deny history, nor did he speculate on what history could or could not be in the development of human knowledge. The conflictual and contradictory ways in which social relations of production are developed are of interest primarily because their effects on the superstructures that develop in society. They have an important affect on the way social relations develop. But these concepts are not merely the result of some internally consistent or logical reduction. They flow from examinations of specific historical periods. In the case of capital, its historical development has been one of institutionalizing itself in order to overcome the social, military, and economic barriers of the feudal era. This was an historical process, with forward and backward motions. First, one class and then another came to the fore or resisted capital's efforts to provide itself with the conditions that would allow it to maximize the surplus value it could expropriate for its own uses. Still relics from the older forms of society persisted, often establishing themselves as barriers that must be overcome by the corporate world, now dominant in world trade.

The domination of capital over people is limited by these historical realities and by the struggles that develop to define and control the direction of social and economic developments in a historical era. There are social relations that do not seem to be related to capital, that seem extraeconomic in nature. Yet even these relics from the past have been influenced by capital's dominance in the workplace. Showing again the power of capital to control every aspect of human existence, Marx writes, "He who can purchase bravery is brave, though a coward. Money is not exchanged for a particular thing, a particular quality, or a specific human faculty, but for the whole objective world of men and nature.''

THE STRUCTURAL ELEMENTS OF PRODUCTION

The means of production refers to the way certain elements of the work process are put together in order to produce commodities in a capitalist system. Balibar was able to extract basic elements in this productive process from Marx's writings: primary relations or connections that operated to control or direct other elements.[7] The primary relations or features of the productive process were the worker, the means and instruments of production, and the materials which were transformed in the labor process into commodities. This latter category contained also the nonworker who appropriates the surplus value of laborers for his own purposes.

Marx, too, was concerned with the ways in which social structures changed through time, considering historical transitions to be important parts of his thinking. But Balibar and Althusser took the position that the modes of production were concepts that could be used in different phases of the development of all societies in human history. This is different from Marx's principle that the modes of production and reproduction of economic life were the ways in which historical epochs could be identified, rather than by their ideological or cultural artifacts. The lineage of kings and princes was an example of traditional forms of history and did not deal with the social and economic conflicts that were the true subject matter of historical science. Historians outside the Marxist tradition divided the past into periods without ever thinking about the assumptions such methods presumed. Human existence was seen as a straight line in time, a series of forward motions that traveled on a linear pathway. Marx, on the other hand, saw the social world as a totality, with each social formation possessing its own inner direction and sources of conflict as defined by the historical context.

Attempts to characterize the production modes of primitive societies using Balibar's concepts were problematic, at best. Lineage-based cultures were organized through kinship groups and traditions that controlled the land or other instruments of production and distribution. Althusser and Balibar had tried to conceptualize the mode of production along structuralist lines: the worker, the object of the work or the process, and the instruments needed to perform the work. The need to transform and control nature created cooperative efforts, which in turn structured the social nature of work and the distribution of the products produced. The ideological structures that developed to support these conditions led to educational training in the family, which had the responsibility of reproducing the language, culture, and social understandings of the kinship group.

Balibar makes the further point that a complicated set of relations exists between these terms, a property connection, as he calls it, and an appropriation one. Yet he is less than clear as to how we can distinguish between these two connections. In the latter, the capitalist takes over the distribution and profits as the natural outcome of his entrepreneurial efforts. Production is seen as a combination of the workers' labor, the instruments and means of production, and the object of labor that transforms the object into a salable commodity. The capitalist is seen as the most important element in the process, as without his organizing of the elements of production, no commodities would be produced. This idea that the capitalist is an indispensable feature of the production process is certainly not a Marxist idea, but it does have consequences for our ideas about the property connection mentioned earlier. That connection means that the capitalist has the power and the legal right to expropriate the surplus value created by the labor of workers in his establishment. It also means that the three elements of production—the production process, distribution, and consumption—are thought of as three separate features of a single process. Marx had already written that the relations of production, which covered all of these constituent elements of the process, were not separate from one another. Production was seen as indissolubly social and material in the same moment. The production process caused commodities to be created at the same instance that it was establishing social relations between the worker and capitalists. Marx saw that the unity of this process was conflictual in nature, because of the class structure it supported in the social world. The conflict was a struggle between workers and capitalists to control the surplus value that was created in the production process. As we have mentioned, Marx made a distinction between the production of value and use value, noting that workers were forced to work more than was necessary for them to reproduce the value of their labor power. The surplus value of their efforts was expropriated or used by the capitalist for his own advantage.

Balibar's antihistoricist concepts of production led him to accept bourgeois ideas about material production. In order to construct universal elements of production, Marx's ideas must be cleansed of their historical materialism and replaced by concepts that are entirely structural and theoretical. History is no longer seen as the beginning and continuation of modes of production; it is now another element in the process, when it is used at all. These ideas have their origins in functionalism, as we have shown in chapters 3 and 4. Production is understood in anatomical, pseudobiological terms. For Balibar and Althusser, production in every age has consisted of invariant elements. Each historical mode is always a combination of these elements in the productive processes, and history is nothing more than their progression from the past to the present. This way of thinking about the modes of production in society provides also a theory of history, as the modes in every era can be compared and distinguished from one another.

A fundamental error appears when we examine further Balibar's notion that production modes in feudal society were dominated by political forces and that ground rent was part of these processes.[8] Marx did discuss other instances of feudal labor, during which time labor and surplus labor were created during the same time frame. But he did not refer to the political level of society as the determinant one in these circumstances. Rather Marx referred to religion, and specifically Catholicism as a major player in the life of persons living in the Middle Ages. Finally, Balibar's structural concepts of production give the economic sphere an autonomy that would be untenable in a Marxist theory.

Balibar's concepts of the political system as the dominant one in feudal society, according to Clarke, is not a Marxist one at all. It has its roots in the ideological structures that justified the bourgeois revolutions of the nineteenth and twentieth centuries and in the classical political economists. These economists tended to regard the status quo as everlasting, and the social relations of production in capitalist society as immutable and ahistorical in nature. This happens because all prehistory is seen as the prelude to capitalism, thus robbing the past of its distinctive and evolutionary features. The classical economists lauded capitalism over feudalism and the past by focusing on the inequities in the distribution processes of such societies, without ever dealing sufficiently with the relations of production. Precapitalist social systems are characterized as arbitrary administrations of the state and the economy, in which the political power continuously intervened on the side of the landed estates. In these writings, the feudal lord becomes nothing more than an entrepreneur or capitalist owning land, using his monopoly of political power to secure and profit from the land he owns. Ideas such as profit and loss, self-employment, and wages are used in these analyses, even though they were neither known nor used by the people who lived through those times.

We should question this idea that the political is determinant either in feudal or modern society. The process of exploitation that has existed in every society has been experienced by individuals in a personal way, but it has been based on class relations and the differing interests of dominant and subordinate groups. We can assume that the class nature of society will perpetuate exploitation of one sort or another, requiring that a state be established that can maintain the advantages and ways of social and economic life preferred by the dominant classes. The state, then, is an instrument and an outgrowth of class relations in society, whether that state is a feudal one protecting the power and dominance of the landed aristocracy or a modern capitalist one protecting the economic rights and privileges of the capitalist class. Within the latter, the state is needed to maintain the conditions of production, that is, the commoditization of labor power and accumulation processes and to provide the ideological institutions that can reproduce the social relations of production in schools and society. The relations between classes in capitalist society are formed in the workplace when the worker accepts his wage contract. This involves the state and its ideological apparatuses, which socialize workers into accepting these social relations of production as natural and reasonable outcomes of the productive process. In feudal society, the state was needed to preserve the subservient condition of the landless peasant and to maintain the legal rights of the dominant classes. Thus the relations of dependence between serfs and landowners was preserved by a state that imposed itself upon the poorer classes, who were utterly dependent upon the largess of those who owned the land they worked. The socialization processes were performed mostly in the family and churches, but they were reinforced by the conditions of life which the peasant or serf found himself in every day.

Balibar's concepts of the mode of production are overly structural, even as he makes allowances for the internal-relatedness of its various elements. The functional needs of the labor process and the nature of the capitalists' control over the production and distribution of commodities are insufficiently treated. The capitalist who uses the worker's surplus labor for his own purposes does not play any role in the actual production processes. Only bourgeois political economists would insert him into the process as an indispensable element, coordinating and controlling the work of laborers. Yet the production process usually has an ideological explanation that justifies it in the eyes of the worker and his employers. In Japan there is the paternalism of the corporate structures and the unity of the group and nation, while in the United States it is the right of entrepreneurs to make a profit. Workers in the latter instance are expected to be grateful to these capitalists, without whom the production process would cease to exist. The worker in Balibar's five invariant elements is a consequence of class societies. As such, they cannot be transported to precapitalist societies where workers and capitalists did not exist.

To summarize: Balibar's emphasis on the structure of the production process gives insufficient weight to historical processes and the ideological weight of linguistic concepts. For Marx, the significance of the productive processes was in the social relations that developed around them, not in the relations between the structural features of production. It is in the way these social relations of production change during their historical life, the way that they are born, live, and die in a never-ending process, that the forms of social reality make themselves known. Social orders ebb and flow, passing on when new forces of production come into being and replace them. This movement of social change was not a technical or mechanical one for Marx, as it seems to be for Balibar. It was the sum total of human actions, actions limited by the historical times and societies in which they occurred. Marx believed that men made their own histories, but they did this in circumstances chosen by others who had lived before them. The social relations of society can be changed, but these changes are limited by the modes of production created in the past.

In contrast to Balibar, Marx believed that a historical approach to social science was imperative. This led him to a critical approach to precapitalist and capitalist systems and an understanding that present-day concepts often distorted realities that existed in the past. The worker in the production process, an indispensable element for Balibar in every instance where work is performed in history, cannot be generalized to include precapitalist societies. The term worker simply did not exist, nor did the concept. People did do work, but they did it in locations, situations, and groups fundamentally different from those in which we see workers doing work in capitalist systems. The worker in capitalist society leaves his home to work in offices or factories where many or most of the people are strangers. In the feudal period, the worker seldom left his family or home, working in the fields or in craft industries organized around familial and kinfolk relations. Neither the craftsman nor the serf hired himself out for wages, and both produced very little surplus value. The relations between these workers and their superiors were very different from the worker–boss relations we see in modern society. Only in the capitalist era has the worker who sells his labor for set periods of time existed. The serf or peasant worked continuously, ordering his daytime activities by the rise and fall of sunlight. Only in capitalist society is the worker thought of as a cost of production, with little or no attention paid to his familial responsibilities and attachments. So the concept of worker can be used only in a system of thought that is ahistorical and unconcerned with what happened or what is happening in the real world. Those who accept Balibar and Althusser's idea that theory is autonomous and apart from social reality will be happy with these ideas. The importance of understanding that the worker is a modern concept and category that cannot be generalized to the past cannot be overstated.

A final example can be taken from the pre–Civil War United States.[9] Slavery was rejected by the North because it contradicted the ideas of free labor and competition between citizens living in a republic. The South, on the other hand, saw slaves as capital. Relations between slaves and masters, who often worked and lived together, created powerful emotional ties that were opposed to good business practices as they had developed in the North and in Europe. There, the worker left his home to work in factories or offices. His labor power was commoditized as a cost of production, but in his life after hours he was free to pursue his personal interests. This was superior to the use of force, because the control that it utilized was a symbolic one accepted by employees and owners alike. Force was used in the South as it had been in other social systems of the past. As a second example, force was used to control the labor of American Indians after Columbus discovered America. But this resulted in the extermination of the indigenous populations in the West Indies and their decimation on the continent. The ideology which supported these genocidal acts stated that Indians were not as human as Europeans were; they were nonbelievers, or heathen, and deserved little or no consideration. Their conversion to Christianity was impossible. The only thing to be done was to enslave them and use their labor power for the good of their masters. Non-Marxian thought has been able to trace the rise and fall of other civilizations, such as the Confederacy or the Spanish colonialists, but it has been unable or unwilling to apply these insights to capitalist systems also. For these thinkers, there has been history in the past but there is no longer to be history for modern capitalism. This ahistorical way of thinking about the present hampers Balibar when he develops his generalized elements of material production.

PRODUCTION IN CAPITALIST AND FEUDAL SOCIETIES

The relations of production in capitalist societies are distinguishable from other forms of exploitation in precapitalist societies because they occur entirely in the area of the workplace.[10] A second distinguishing characteristic, as Marx has shown, is that the exploitation happens without any overt forms of coercion, because of the time and space requirements of production and the ways in which surplus values are accumulated. It is difficult or impossible for an individual worker to know at what moment of the working day he has stopped working to replace the value of his consumption, or labor costs, and when he is producing surplus value that will be used by his capitalist employer for his own purposes.[11] The processes of accumulation, production, and consumption are so complicated they are usually misunderstood by workers, when they think about these things at all. This makes it possible for the employer to make his exchange offer to workers as one which is reasonable and equitable, that is, a wage for the labor a man or woman can produce in a forty-hour week. The worker has access to the production-distribution processes of the economy only through his wage contract.

Althusser and Balibar contrast the way things were produced in capitalist and feudal societies.[12] In the latter system, the difference between necessary labor time and surplus labor time was more evident. The feudal serf worked his rented land to meet his needs and those of his family. But he was also obliged to pay for his right to work the landlord's land by performing extra labor or by paying rent, because the serf did not own the land he worked; his only access was through the permission given and conditions laid down by the property's owners. The authors use this contrast in the modes of exploitation to account for the different social classes and methods of dominance that characterized these two modes of production. In capitalist society, the domination and exploitation of workers occurred only in the workplace. Other social formations were given relative autonomy, so that the individual could separate his work and personal lives as though they were completely apart from one another. But in feudal society, the laborer could see when he was working for his own subsistence and when his labor was being appropriated by the landowner. This meant that extra-economic forms of coercion were needed if surplus value was to be gotten from serfs. Thus class relations were more rigid and unchanging, and the right to wage war was vested in the nobility and landowning classes. Political and economic force were also in the hands of this ruling class, and education was withheld from the children of the poorer classes in society.

Althusser and Balibar declare that Marx's historical materialism provided scholars with the "elements of scientific knowledge" and a "true theoretical science, and therefore an abstract science."[13] They reclaim and reinterpret such basic concepts as the "mode of production, social formation, determined in the last instance by the economic and the different levels of social formations themselves." In their hands, ideology, politics, and education now became transhistorical and cross-cultural concepts that were prevalent in all social formations represented in the history of humankind. They sought to develop an abstract theoretical science from Marx's work, even though that work was grounded in historical materialism and an emphasis on the real and the specific in social analysis. Of course, they realized that the structural elements, or universal concepts as they called them, were not able to provide sufficient theoretical understandings without adding certain specific social formations characteristic of a particular age.

From this we can see that the schools that capitalism establishes have a primary interest: the development of an ideology and culture that makes it natural for students to accept the appropriation of the worker's surplus value as normal and natural, as part of an economic system that has always existed in one form or another. Teachers must ignore the problems that develop in the production processes themselves, teaching little about union movements of the past and present. Relations between workers and their employers must also be ignored, and the effects of these associations on the social and political relations discussed in a case-by-case method, when they are discussed at all. The question of how goods are distributed and what happens to those who do not possess effective demand is seldom made a part of the curriculum. The ideology of schooling insists that students accept the economic system without question, that they treat strangers with suspicion, and that they accept the superiority of the economic and social system within which they live. Ideas such as plutocracy and the ways in which unequal economic power distorts democratic structures is almost never broached by teachers (or professors). In part, this is because teachers (and professors) are products of the educational production of these state schools and have often never thought deeply about these matters.

Returning to Marx's theories, we may ask: Can they help us understand the transformation that took place in the transition from feudalism to capitalism? Can they provide more than historical explanations of such social transformations? Can Marxism provide us with a coherent theory of personality development as it occurred during the past few centuries? To answer these questions we turn now to the work of Ferdinand Tonnies.

GEMEINSCHAFT UND GESELLSCHAFT

The work of Ferdinand Tonnies gave rise to new insights into the transformation of human identity that occurred in the transition from precapitalist to capitalist society. These were concerned with the alienation individuals experienced in the movement from simple barter to increased competition in the marketplace, from the agrarian world of the past to world trade, with its endless need to reproduce capital as surplus value.[14] Writing in the late 1800s, Tonnies was able to see that man was becoming estranged in a world of rapid transition, that he was a lonely individual living in mass communities. The primary relations of gemeinschaft were being lost because of new changes in the way individuals lived together. The values of family and community were being supplanted by those of individualism and cosmopolitanism; the different needs, interests, desires, and attitudes of the avaricious capitalist now held sway. This led to less cooperation in the workplace and more competition. The values and world outlook of capitalism became prevalent, creating cities of unlimited size and presenting humanity with a new phenomenon, the eclipse of gemeinschaft relationships of family and community and the ascendancy of useful or contractual relations that Tonnies labeled the gesellschaft.[15] Yet the gemeinschaft had characterized human history from its beginnings. Its essence was and is the family, especially the mother–child relationship. It exists without awareness or intention on the part of its members. Individuals in families are united as persons rather than for their usefulness in attaining particular goals. Gemeinschaft signifies the unity of kinship groups living and working in the same house, the same village. It evolves from the sharing of common ancestors and a way of life that binds members into close-knit groups within which members' life activities occur. The gemeinschaft concept could also be thought of as including neighborhood dwellers and people who shared the same customs and beliefs. It could also encompass friends who come together through affection, similar likes and dislikes, and occupations.[16]

In the period when gemeinschaft predominated, individuals centered their lives around their families, communities, and social estates. In the process, private property and money economies remained undeveloped. Tonnies agreed with Marx that the social structure of capitalism had broken down these strong communal organizations of the precapitalist period. The individual had become more isolated and alone; human relationships were being supplanted by useful associations. With this social transformation there was a lessening of the individual's commitment to the values, ideas, and roles of precapitalist society.

Tonnies, writing during a period when many of these changes were still occurring, made the further point that the tendencies toward gesellschaft created a new kind of individual who was concerned about himself and what belonged to him. This new person was more reflective, calculating his advantages in every relationship into which he entered. "To him everything becomes a means to an end . . . his relationships to other men, and thus to associations of all kinds, begins to change."[17] In the new era, the individual appears upon the stage of history separate and apart from his family and community. His contacts with other human beings are established only when they are deemed useful. The close bonds of the gemeinschaft period are replaced by the ascendant gesellschaft.

The triumph of the gesellschaft, of the contractual relationship entered into with prior calculation for the attainment of mutual ends, forces people to interact with one another segmentally, with only a part of the personality. This fragmented personality shows only that part of itself that relates to the specific demands of organized economic or educational activities. The force that supports these types of associations is the individual's gains and aspirations in capitalist society. In such a society, as we have seen, the control of the tools of production are lost and the sense of community that human beings have had since the dawn of time is shattered by the tension and isolation individuals feel in mass society. Without these primary groups, the individual experiences an identity crisis, a loss of self-knowledge and an inability to achieve meaningful associations within the void of the gesellschaft. Each sees himself or herself as buyer or seller, employer or employee; and the activities of each become obsessed with processes of commodity accumulations.[18]

These insights into the movement from gemeinschaft to gesellschaft began to change and become more insistent in our own time.[19]

These insights into the movement from gemeinschaft to gesellschaft allowed Tonnies to develop two polar types of human will or personality: Wesenwille, or natural or integrated will associated with gemeinschaft relationships, and Kurwille, or will shaped by rational weighing of ends and means associated with gesellschaft relationships. Wesenwille is the impulsive expression of the drives and impulses of human beings. It corresponds to their natural likes and dislikes, their natural dispositions, and signifies the individual's will as it encompasses the process of thinking. Kurwille, on the other hand, is conditioned by rational thought and the assessment of means and ends. It assesses the pros and cons and signifies the person's thinking as it includes his will as one of many elements to be considered in making a rational decision. These two forms of will are central to Tonnies' theories of personal development, even though he believed that most individuals were combinations of these polar types. In recent history, however, Kurwille has become predominant. Commenting on the use of Kurwille and the nature of labor in capitalist society, Tonnies wrote that, to a large degree, the work of the masses of individuals has become impersonal and unsatisfying. "The satisfaction which most of us find in our work is not inherent in the occupational activities which we carry out; it is found primarily in the pay envelope . . . the numbers of hours put in . . . work for extrinsic end . . . to avail the individual of means which have no inner relationship to his life and its goals. . . . Kurwille divorces means from ends."[20]

The ascendancy of gesellschaft has weakened the sense of community that human beings have always experienced in the past. It has created an isolated individual who lives and works in increasingly depersonalized cities and suburbs. Gesellschaft man, detached from his family and community, floats in and out of relationships. He participates in corporate structures that he is powerless to control and seems incapable of replacing the traditional values of the precapitalist period with new ones that will restore a sense of meaningfulness to his life.

A critique of Tonnies' elegant theories must deal with his glorification of the precapitalist social order as a "golden age" during which individuals lived in greater safety and security than they enjoy today. The idea views serfdom or the peasant-landowner relations as beneficent social relations in which men viewed one another not as commodities, but as whole human beings. Work was not fragmented, as it is today. Peasants or artisans were able to complete most aspects of their work and could take pride in their accomplishments. These benign pictures of the past ignore the grinding disease and poverty that characterized the lives of the peasant classes and also ignores the military, political, and legal force used to maintain the class structures of these precapitalist systems. Referring to our criticism of Balibar earlier in this chapter, we believe that workers in different social systems cannot be compared, if we mean to show a higher degree of satisfaction in one or the other systems. Serfs worked within a familial and kinship structure foreign to most modern employees, but that structure was more arbitrary and less profitable. They may have lived in a gemeinschaft, but it was a set of relations that kept them impoverished and without hope. Wars may have been less destructive in this period, as Tonnies wrote, but they were continuous. Barter may have been more simple, but it existed only because mankind had not yet perfected his abilities to communicate and traverse large distances. The supposition that humans who live in a gesellschaft suffer more than people did in the past certainly needs further examination. And the ideal types of kurwille and wesenwille are overly functional in their construction. Of course, Tonnies wrote that most persons were a blend of the two, depending upon the situation they found themselves in. Still, the unification of social systems theory and psychology did point the way for us. Men and women in modern society have become more calculating in their thinking and less related to their familial roots, because, as Tonnies noted, capital needs individuals whom it can hire for its production needs. These individuals must be willing to relocate themselves in a way that would have been difficult for serfs, peasants or artisans. They need the individuals who have difficulty communicating with others and who know little about the economic system within which they work.

THE PAST WE HAVE LOST

Tonnies' world of gemeinschaft had a commercial as well as agrarian side. A business such as a bakery was likely to be located in the house of the baker himself. Everyone who worked in the bakery was likely to be a family member or an apprentice. All of them ate their meals together and slept in the house. These people lived and worked together as a family. The owner was an entrepreneur or master who was also the head of the family. He was the actual parent of some of the workers and a surrogate father to other members of the establishment. His wife was worker, mother, and partner. She bought the food and managed the servants and the household. She was subordinate to the husband because she was a woman, even though she was the mother of his children. Apprentices were treated like extra sons. Their clothing, food, education, and welfare was the concern of the "father." They in turn owed him their obedience, allegiance, and dependency until they were twenty-one.

This world was not the paradise Tonnies speaks of in his writings. There was inequality, intolerance, and war on a grand scale. Economic oppression and exploitation were more severe and constant. Employment arrangements were abusive and enslaved many in an encompassing manner. Before the coming of capitalism and world trade, people endured deep oppression because they thought such social and economic forms were unchangeable and ever-lasting. There was no recourse for injustices, there was no hope for better times. Economic relationships were intertwined with familial ones. Both were regulated by rigid codes and traditions and by religious precepts, which made for a very stable society. The power of gemeinschaft communications was a powerful one, forcing the discontented and frustrated to despair of ever reconciling their grievances.

Everyone lived within twenty miles of their birth site. They lived in families that knew everything about them. Their marriages were arranged for economic reasons, and marriage was the only way to enter into full membership in the family. Their work took place in human-sized establishments. When the owner died, the establishment often died too. Few of the adults or apprentices went out of the house; older persons lived and died in their own homes. There was little or no mingling with persons from different social origins or backgrounds.

In the agrarian sector, each farm was worked by a family in much the same way as the bakery. Indentured or free servants lived on the farm until they were of age and ready for marriage. If they were landless men and women from landless families, they became cottagers or what Americans called sharecroppers in the modern-day South. Farmers paid wages or fed their workers in lieu of pay. Wages were set by local authorities, and day laborers were symbolically united with the farm family by eating meals with them.[21]

EFFECTS ON THE SCHOOL

Finally, something more must be said about the effects of the economy on educational systems. One important innovation, the establishment of high schools in the United States in the first decades of this century, can serve as a case study. The nature and pedagogy of these high schools remained in dispute for many years after they were established. Most educators agreed they should be training grounds for adult life. But there agreement ended. Some thought high school should prepare students for college as it had done in the past. Others believed it should train urban and immigrant youth for the workplace. In 1890, only 6.7 percent of the population was in secondary schools; only 10–20 percent actually graduated. By the 1920s, a high school education was universally demanded by industry and the states of the Union. Old curriculum areas of Latin, Greek, and theology were replaced by more secular subject matter. Still, two-thirds of those entering secondary schools failed to graduate; approximately one-third of them left before completing the second year.[22]

What myths and ideologies attached themselves to this sudden expansion of secondary education? Foremost among them was the idea that the schools would be "people's colleges," bridging the gap between elementary education and college training. School authorities assured immigrant and working-class parents that the resources of the state would be used to provide youngsters with equal opportunity in schools and in the workplace. People of all classes were welcomed and promised an education that would meet their needs to assimilate into the society and the labor market. To immigrants and workers, the high school offered industrial and craft training; to merchants and businessmen, bookkeeping and typing skills; to the college-bound, logic, language, and science; to the wealthy, a liberal education that would keep them separate from the other classes in society. To those who were concerned with democracy, the high school promised youth understandings and insights that would help them to become informed citizens. To those who hungered after economic advancement, they promised a discipline that would prepare youth to perform their work effectively once they were adults. Those were the values of the system. However, the reality of the high school itself was quite different. While it was advertised as a movement toward greater equality and democracy, its own structures were autocratic, its instructional methods arbitrary and impositional in nature. The organizational needs of mass institutions forced teachers and administrators to become obsessed with problems of order and control, mirroring some of the problems industry was facing during this period in its development.

Secondary education was encouraged during these first decades as a way of counterbalancing the lack of industrial skills of urban poor and immigrant workers. It was meant to deal with their poor attitudes toward work and toward the economic system generally. It was instituted to safeguard the American system during the period after World War I when changes in technology, bureaucracy, and urban life caused confusion and discontent in the working classes of society. The idea of state and economic leaders was simple: place urban and immigrant youth in surroundings where they could be in constant contact with ideas associated with the workplace—skills in working, attending, honesty, punctuality, discipline, and so on.

Coercion was apparent at the outset. Legal requirements forced youngsters to attend, getting them out of the crowded labor market for a number of years. Teenagers were confined in isolated, enormous structures. Their bodily movements were carefully controlled, and their lack of individual rights was the most visible sign of the true nature of these state agencies. The power to command, to direct, to force obedience—these were the values that the workplace demanded of its employees. High schools were now agencies of social constraint, which operated under the guise and ideology of democratic institutions. But youth could not disrupt or resign without facing stern penalties and discrimination when they sought work in the labor market. They were under total domination and control for a part of each weekday, much as they would be when they sold their labor power to employers when they reached adulthood. The pedagogy and morality of the business classes combined to civilize the young and teach them to accept the economic system as it was and to accept their place in it, also.

These high schools performed important functions for American society during a period when it was being transformed from a predominantly agrarian society to an industrial one. Students were confined and sorted into successful and unsuccessful students. Then they were socialized over many years to accept the organizational identities given to them by the schools. They were taught that the present economic system is immutable, logical, and impossible to change because it reflects the realities of human nature. They were instructed in the language and culture of a stratified culture, and those who completed their schoolwork were duly certified.

The work of the high schools was to perform these social tasks for the state and the economy. The military and penal methods of the past were refined and used again. Coercion was still the dominant form of interaction between teachers and students, but it was rendered impersonal by bureaucratic practices and a commonly held view that teachers were overly directive, not because they were bossy, but because they were concerned for the welfare of their students. This made it impossible for students to vent their anger and emotions openly, even when they were frustrated and humiliated in these mass institutions. The state requirement that all students attend these people's colleges led to legions of unprepared youngsters who failed and dropped out as soon as they were able to.

What did educators believe were the moral understandings associated with work in capitalist society? How did these beliefs affect the schoolwork they presented to their students? School teachers believed that schoolwork and industrial labor possessed a disciplinary and constraining force that was essential to the functioning of organizations in modern life. For that reason, business and high schools were characterized by schedules and locations that were separate from the living quarters of workers and students. In the high schools, teachers demanded greater student attentiveness to the work at hand, preparing youth for the workplace. They urged teenagers to show greater concern and a sense of obligation when doing the essentially meaningless schoolwork placed before them. Through secondary schooling, students were taught to respect the authority structures and economic system of the nation. They learned to submit to the authority of the teacher without thinking about what they were being asked to do. Thus schooling prepared individuals for the authoritarian workplace rather than the democratic political structures of the larger American system.

Schoolwork was performed in isolated settings, mirroring the factories and offices of the business world. It was imposed on teenagers to facilitate the creation of an obedient work force that accepted the status quo as "natural" and just. It was a training that sought to limit diversity, forcing immigrant and urban poor youngsters to submit to order as it was interpreted by schoolteachers. Its primary goal was to provide physical and mental constraints that limited the freedom and aspirations of teenagers who were preparing to enter the labor market.

Students were separated from one another by their attainments. Their civil status, as defined by law, was that of ward of the state when they were inside school buildings. Freedom of movement or thinking were disallowed, and the schooling experience was presented to students in moralistic and patriotic terms that sought to legitimate the coercive and impositional behaviors of schoolteachers.

We may summarize briefly the relationships between capitalism and schooling, with a special reference to the American educational system. Capitalism, since its inception, has been a development of European nations; in other areas of the world it came later and was involved with imitation and adaptation.

In order for this system of capitalism to work it must bring workers out of their homes and agrarian settings; it must force them to sell their labor power. To do this is to make labor and laborers a cost of production, subject to the laws of the free market of capitalist economies. Labor is another thing that is brought together and exploited like capital or land by capitalists who venture their capital in the search for profit. Inexpensive labor costs are a practical goal of capitalists, who must compete with one another for scarce resources and customers.

To the degree that workers can be made to act less human and more like a commodity, the capitalist is free to pursue his goal of higher profits. Therefore, the good worker is one who is taught to obey his superiors and to do his work in a machinelike way.

From this we can see that the schools that capitalism establishes have a primary interest: the development of an ideology and culture that makes it natural for students to accept their role as workers and citizens in a plutocracy. This method is superior to the use of force because control is symbolic, deeply internalized and accepted by employees. Force was used to control the labor of American Indians after Columbus colonized America, but this force resulted in the extermination of these indigenous populations in the West Indies and in their decimation on the continent. The ideology that supported these genocidal actions claimed that Indians were not human beings as Europeans were: They were nonbelievers who deserved little or no consideration. Their conversion to Christianity was impossible. The only thing to be done with them was to enslave them and use their labor power for the good of the masters. In Europe, another ideology was used to exploit the labor of white women and children.[23] It was believed that they were in danger of being tempted by the devil because of idleness. They were to suffer poor working conditions in order to save their souls; their suffering was what awaited all human beings in this world or the next.

The ideology of the schools followed those of business, presenting different working-class groups in stereotypical ways that set them apart from one another. Sometimes, as with Afro-American slaves in the past, the very humanity of a group is called into question. At other times, their innate intelligence and abilities are called into question and demeaned as subhuman or worse.

In the schools that trained workers, there was much similarity between their norms and those of the workplace. The student, like the worker or inmate, did not know what was best for him; he did not know what he was supposed to do once he was inside the institution. This ignorant condition was the basis upon which instruction or reformation was provided by those in authority. It also had a secondary effect: the ignorant students, workers, or inmates were also less worthy persons than those who instructed them or guided their behavior. Discipline practices became increasingly important as the size of high schools increased dramatically. Three important practices deserve mention here:

1. *No talking.* Schooling had an antisocial bias that reflected the mores of the workplace. Workers were asked not to talk to one another because talking meant that they paid less attention to the work they were supposed to be doing. Prohibitions against talking or moving without permission also found their counterpart in the demands of the workplace. The public humiliation of students, the sarcasm of teachers were meant to enforce these rules of behavior in classrooms and had the effect of separating teachers and students into two opposing groups, similar to those of workers and management. Students were expected to work much of the day in silence and unison on an uninteresting and irrelevant curriculum, preparing them for the world of work again. Constraints on the bodily movements of students reduced them to automatons and robots, the preferred types of labor in the mass industries that were widespread in the economic sector. The one-way dialogue of teachers stunted the powers of speech and reason in their students, making them less able to question the conditions of their schooling or those in the adult society. As with workers in mass industries, the general response of many students became one of increasing indifference as their schooling identities challenged the personal ones they had developed in their families and communities. They were punished for disobedience, poor work or truancy, smoking, talking, and so on. They were encouraged to be more forthcoming in their schoolwork, more punctual in their habits, more willing to obey the rules and to limit their movements as teachers demanded.

2. *Discipline by imitation in the high school.* Youth were observed by teachers and were made aware of this continuing scrutiny. Students soon learned to imitate the behaviors of older students. In that way they tended to blend into the situation. These were important lessons of schooling, not written into curriculum guides. The socialization and discipline of youth demanded imitation and uniformity, as they did in mass economic institutions. Youth were asked to ape their elders, to come to see the school world and the economic system through the eyes of predecessors

who had accepted the status quo and its legitimate authority to direct their activities.

3. *Discipline by constant evaluation in the high school.* By confronting youth with what they did not know through a series of lessons, examinations, and confrontations in classrooms, students were taught to accept a view of themselves that had been constructed by school authorities. Any teacher in the building had the right and duty to observe, judge, or stop any students anywhere they encountered them. These rights were based on the teachers' status in the school community and had their echo in the rights of management in industry. Discipline in schooling was a socialization method that prepared youth for their future roles in the labor market.

To the no-talking rule, discipline by imitation, and constant evaluations must be added a fourth structure of discipline: the legitimation of the high school teachers' expertise as instructors of youth. As it carried with it the idea of teaching as a "calling," a service provided to society, it tended to blind students and parents to the stratification work that teachers performed in the name of education. An ideological understanding of the teacher–student relationship was thus reaffirmed. Teachers were persons who cared enough about youngsters to teach them, to correct them, and to provide a realistic evaluation of their achievement and abilities. The altruistic basis for teacher behavior was thus strengthened, because these people were giving up higher pay and better positions in order to perform a social service.

6

The Social Relations of Educational Production

In the advanced industrial nations, educational systems are involved, not with knowledge, but with ideological practice. It is in the theory of ideology that educational systems can best be understood. This follows from schooling's preoccupation with language and values, which must be transferred from one generation to the next in an orderly and predictable fashion. For as we have shown, the role of schooling in capitalist society is to produce individuals who cannot understand their relationship to the social order within which they live, learn, and work. To do this, a cultural arbitrary and pedagogic practice are used to reproduce a stratified economic and social system. Every attempt of schools to represent the world is, by definition, doomed to failure. Such attempts are ideological, or imaginary in nature, and cause individuals to misrecognize themselves and their relations to others. All attempts to use language to represent the real world necessarily misrepresent that world. As this is the essence of schooling in mass society, educational systems, which rely upon such representations, must be labelled as ideological state institutions. The product is socialized individuals who sees themselves and the world ideologically. Students are encouraged to believe that what they are taught in classrooms represents valid knowledge of the economy, the state, and the society. Educational systems pretend to be steeped in realism and empiricism, seeking to generate in students an acceptance of their teachings as legitimate and correct.[1] Thus teachers talk about how the world is and evaluate how successful students are in their ability to comprehend that world. Such teachers form a hierarchy in their profession and in schools. At the top are those who teach the higher grade levels and at universities; at the bottom are elementary schoolteachers and those who teach the children of the poorer classes. In each instance, however, students and parents are asked to accept the efforts of teachers as adequate and real. Through this willingness to recognize state schools as the purveyors of valid knowledge comes a second consequence: the acceptance by students of the social relations of educational and material production as ahistorical, unchangeable realities that must be accommodated and never questioned. These social relations come to be understood as legitimate and natural structures that have been fashioned by the needs of human nature and by society itself.

THE STRUCTURE OF LANGUAGE

The structure of language plays a defining role in educational production and in the establishment of institutional identities for teachers and students. Seeking to understand this structure of language is not a new approach to learning. What is new is the coalescence of social science disciplines around the study of human communications and linguistic systems.[2] Language has been divided into the study of grammar and its patterns and the acts of speaking in situations such as the classroom. By studying a language as a complete system, structuralists have come to understand that structure and totality determine every other facet within it. Changing any part alters every other part in the system. The precedence of the totality over its parts is an important feature of structuralist thought and fits in well with the internal-relatedness theories discussed earlier.

Also, the structure and meaning of language in classrooms is never to be sought in observable reality. Rather, the search for what lies below or behind the surface should be the goal of study. What is happening between teachers and students as they communicate with one another? The organizations that govern and define linguistic communications are unconscious or structured by unseen forces outside the classroom. The teacher speaks without consciously being aware of the grammar or speech laws she applies at a given moment during the school day. A particular language is spoken in schools even when the students are from diverse linguistic and cultural backgrounds. Certain features of every language are invariant and capable of being transposed into mathematical sign systems.

A problem: structural studies of language are often ahistorical and the processes seen as invariant and ever-present givens. Language cannot be isolated from the social and economic system within which it is used, nor can its historical contexts be ignored. An unmasking of the texts and curriculum of state schools would necessarily be followed by an unmasking of the symbolic violence inherent in pedagogical actions. Would working-class and lower-middle class families support such an education, especially if it led to a breakdown of the competitive ethos of schooling that they have accepted? Could such unmaskings be done if pedagogic action and texts were shrouded by ideological effects, if they made it difficult for students and teachers to see the ideological production that disguised itself as education? The idea that the ordinary teacher and student might not be able to participate in these intellectual reappraisals cannot be dismissed lightly. If traditional forms of schooling reproduce the social relations of educational production by making them familiar and recognizable to teachers, students and parents, then an attempt to disrupt such schooling would be dysfunctional for them and for society. The production of educational knowledge has, as one of its historical functions, the reaffirmation of class divisions through the dissemination of ideology. This, in turn, teaches poorer classes their inferior condition and prepares them to accept the successes of others as deserved. Therefore, the attempt to move away from traditional pedagogy and symbolic violence would have a deleterious effect on teachers and on the socialization processes the schools are mandated to reproduce. How can we change the competitive ethos of schooling when it is accepted by the majority of citizens and functions throughout society? How can schooling be made more equitable when it uses a language and cultural discourse familiar only to the dominant classes?

THE TEACHER'S DILEMMA

The teacher who comes to teaching "to help children" must use the approved curriculum guides and linguistic practices to retain a position. But these materials generate ideological insights that cause students to accept institutional definitions of themselves, their families, and their potential in schools and in the labor market. The teacher, wishing to raise the consciousness of students, might engage them in a learning experience that helps them to cope with their own experiences. In order to do so, the teacher must find a way to avoid using this language of oppression. One approach could be to make students aware just how approximate knowledge of social reality is once it is transformed into language. This could be done by studying how textbooks and spoken language signify realty and then listing the many features of observed situations that are omitted from these communications. Where the traditional educational training never contemplates its own practices and production methods, the nontraditional approach would make them a subject of study and discourse. The teacher might want to study how traditional educational production led to ideological effects, showing students how and why they were controlled and manipulated in state schools. This would change schooling radically, making it a study of itself and the ways in which it stratifies and passes on knowledge through language and cultural systems. The reality that is transposed into signification codes and, ultimately, into the students' stream of consciousness, cannot reveal the object world. Social reality, especially, is too large, too conflict-ridden, too unconscious to be grasped in its entirety. But studies of schooling's practices and social functions can open up new levels of truth and understanding for students. Whereas traditional schooling is deliberately irrelevant to the lives of students and their families, forcing youngsters to assume the role of the ignorant and unworthy "learner," the nontraditional approach could study why this irrelevance is enforced by the state and educational authorities. The student would no longer be a passive consumer of prepackaged modules of state-validated knowledge. Now she would be the cocreator of her daily classroom experiences, focusing on the sign systems and cultures that are influenced by dominant groups and classes. Teachers would no longer have a privileged position in the classroom, and the separation between teachers and students would decrease.

Of course, this concept of traditional education is stereotypical. Every curriculum adopted in state schools will eventually become subservient to the needs of the dominant classes that fund the educational system. Knowledge validated by schools ultimately will serve the interests of the state and economy. All knowledge of social reality places limits on what teachers and students can understand, even as they pretend to tell all. No curriculum can be taught in precisely the same way, so that its intended meanings are passed on as they were originally designed. A nonideological approach to pedagogic acts and curriculum might find itself contradicting everything that was accepted as the truth by the members of society, until there was nothing that could be stated with certainty. This might prove to be less valuable to students, who often seek answers to the vexing problems in their school and personal lives.

Our commonsense understandings of schooling make it easier for us to understand the teacher–pupil relationship as it is taking place in state schools. This helps us to see the social conflict between them once the teacher begins pedagogic actions, to teach them the state syllabus. We can use these understandings to think about how these experiences are affecting teachers and students as they work together in classrooms. Teachers sitting in front of their classes might understand that a struggle is taking place, a struggle for dominance. They might also believe that if they were firm in the beginning, if they pressed their case until they prevailed, all would be well. On another level of understanding, however, they could question their feelings as they tried to force students to submit to their right to decide everything inside the classroom. They might decide that, in the interests of order and control, they must insist that students seat themselves quietly, put their clothing away when their rows are called, and so on. They might also insist that the silence rules be enforced during attendance, during assignments and classwork, when they are speaking, or when they write on the blackboard. They could point to the materials that must be covered during the class meetings, asking the students to accept their judgment of them every moment of the school day. This is not to deny that some teachers will come to see their work as difficult and unpleasant even as they force youngsters to attend to curricula unrelated to anything in their lives. It is to focus attention on the submissive responses of students that are required by state schools. It is to recognize how teachers might justify the large numbers of children from minority backgrounds who fail to succeed in the classroom. It is also related to the aggressiveness they may exhibit when resistance flares up and their authority and right to control the situation is challenged. On one level, teachers may see their failure as personal, but this may lead to greater inflexibility and stubbornness as they identify more and more with the educational system that employs them.

Teachers new to the profession may accept the idea that, at first, the personal front presented to students would have to be consistent and severe. Listening to the advice of older teachers, they would learn that they were not supposed to give in to the childish demands of students, even if their actions were disliked. They might think more about their inexperience and decide to impose their definitions of the classroom situation no matter what the cost. These teachers might come to accept the idea that controlling children would be easier if they were given busy work, if they made constant demands on the students' time and energy.

These kind of insights can place a strain on teachers and their self-concept, causing them to be tense and demanding in front of students. They may find themselves constantly thinking about what to say to students, what to tell them to do at different moments during the school day. Experiencing their first difficulties, they may have nightmares about losing control over the pupils.[3] The teachers may decide to keep these pupils busy and off-balance, lest they ask why, and to keep them guessing about how they will be graded.

We can extend this analysis to other, veteran teachers who are working in inner-city schools that experience failure as their daily fare. Teachers may come to see observable effects of such work as they succumb to the routines and demands of custodial educational practices. Often, they become less adaptable, less amiable, and less willing to use humor in their classrooms.

Some teachers may feel a deadening of their intellectual capacities as they age, exhibiting teacherish ways of thinking and acting outside their classrooms. They tend to seek consensus on important matters and lack adaptability or intellectual curiosity. Perhaps this is why teaching is thought of as a profession that tends to narrow the scope of its members. The ways teachers approach students are much more stereotyped and rigidly organized than the clinical settings in courtrooms and other professions.

These experiences in inner-city schools force teachers to teach basic skills year after year, without helping students to go beyond the simple skills these pedagogic actions require.

Finally, teachers do not see themselves as workers, even though they earn wages and sometimes join unions. Usually, they are solitary, spending most of their time enclosed in classrooms without seeing other adults. The situation of teachers is a segregated one in which the social class position of students is seldom thought about. Teachers play a paramount role in reproducing the social relations of educational production so that schools can maintain themselves from one generation to the next. In the longer term, they also produce the workers who will labor in the factories and offices of the next generation. They teach the linguistic and cultural imperatives of the state, committing symbolic violence on children of the minority and poor and weeding out as failures those who do not merit promotion to higher grades or better-paying occupations later in life. But the ways teachers approach students and the practices they use are certainly influenced by outside social and economic forces. They are also influenced by traditions of dominance and submission that characterize relations between teachers and students. These methods of keeping children dependent and in their place have economic origins, and they are required by the peculiar needs for order and control that develop in classrooms and workplaces. The ways teachers act in classrooms have become a part of the folklore and literature of Western society. But what teachers teach and how their work is evaluated is also important. If teachers developed insights into the work they are doing for society, they might be less willing to accept things as they find them in schools. They might be more willing to change if they knew that their behaviors in classrooms generated anger and confusion in students, making it more difficult for their students to succeed. The force of ideology needs to be considered whenever teachers begin to think about what they are doing and why they work in such massive, impersonal institutions. Knowledge is socially conditioned and needs to be produced in situations, and amid social relations, that mimic those of the economic and social sector. The differences between traditional and nontraditional pedagogies is not the difference between various linguistic interpretations of the past, but between those which discuss their suppositions and biases openly and those which do not. Certainly the texts of most state schools do not disclose their biases. But teachers can do this themselves, using the texts as ideological constructions that possess a certain amount of truth while ignoring their suppositions and distortions. It is easier for students and teachers to interact in traditional forms of classroom pedagogy than in nontraditional ones. They are more familiar with the traditional and more uncertain of the mores and values of the nontraditional. All education that is familiar and easy to understand is suspect, because it generally implies a disinterest in the structure of these communications and biases of their communicators.

THE SOCIAL DYNAMICS OF RACISM

The Afro-American student, among others, suffers from these ideological stereotypes and practices of schooling and society.[4] Afro-Americans, with some exceptions, have attempted to assimilate themselves into the wider American culture for more than 400 years. In this respect, they are like other immigrant groups that have migrated during the past from other parts of Europe, Asia, and South America. However, their separate world has endured, because the white ruling classes in the United States have opposed their assimilation. This opposition showed itself when teaching a slave to read was an offense punishable by death. It continued in our period as segregation. Segregation limits the ability of individuals in different races to communicate and understand one another. It is an instrument for developing stereotypes, which are often used to justify discriminatory practices. For centuries the relations between whites and Afro-Americans were between white upper-class landowners or capitalists and Afro-American servants and field hands. More recently it has come to include capitalists in the northeast and west and Afro-Americans who sought work in the factories and offices of large corporations.

As the schools are themselves a product of this segregation system, they often do not teach students about segregation and its effects on themselves and their families. Keeping the races apart in residential neighborhoods and schools makes it impossible for people to see their common humanity. Afro-Americans are forced to pray separately, even as a few churches move away from strict segregation on the basis of race. They are buried in separate cemeteries, play in separate playgrounds, live in a separate but parallel world seldom seen by white Americans.

What is race prejudice, and why has it persisted for so many centuries? It is a social attitude taught by ideological state apparatuses such as the schools, the family, the state, and the church. It is propagated so that a race or ethnic group may be stereotyped and stigmatized in the mind of the public. It justifies the practices of racial and ethnic discrimination that occur in the business world. Afro-Americans are segregated and persecuted so that they may be more easily exploited in the labor market. Unemployment has always been twice as high in this group than among corresponding white workers, and these figures do not tell the full story. Afro-Americans have been members of the reserve army of labor so important to capitalist society, where the search for cheap labor is ongoing and where the business cycle has been an uncontrollable constant. During bad times, this group has borne the brunt of layoffs. Race prejudice is a socio-attitudinal way of explaining away the exploitation of the labor of Afro-Americans by referring to their supposed inferiorities and deficiencies. The goals of race prejudice are constraining ones that seek to limit opportunities. They seek to prevent Afro-Americans from assimilating into the white culture and insist they remain as they have always been, part of a group outside the mainstream of white America.

Children are likely to experience discrimination and prejudice at an early age, before they enter schools. The schools, of course, have been bastions of segregation for more than 400 years in the United States, and since the Civil War they have practiced and preached segregation. After 1954, when the Supreme Court mandated integration in the nation's schools, the judicial demands were resisted throughout the country; and today the inner-city school districts in the United States are more segregated than ever. Children are asked to attend segregated schools, where the culture and language are suffused with discriminatory attitudes and practices. These experiences are part of the socialization training of state schools, during which persons from different races and cultures learn how different they really are when compared to the dominant white culture.

The abuse that Afro-American children experience in schools can sometimes be akin to what working-class white children experience. But the experiences are not identical, by any means. Maintaining social distance is quite different from maintaining racial differences, although some of the effects are similar. Discrimination against youngsters because of their race causes severe tension and anguish in children who experience it.

The textbooks read in state schools seldom show Afro-Americans in favorable ways, and children soon learn that their racial background is not valued by their teachers and schools. They learn that teachers judge them by their work in class and by the color of their skin. The suffering this causes is quite severe, as it conflicts with the language constructions that identified children before they entered such schools. Children may become self-conscious of their color in such situations, reproaching their families and themselves for the experiences they have in classrooms. When these incidents are added to those that develop in families which are struggling to survive on the fringes of an exploitative labor market, loneliness and self-rejection often result.

The outcome of these social-psychological pressures to conform to a culture and society that will not allow them to successfully do so produces a self-deflating effect. Schooling seeks to teach Afro-American children their lack of importance in the educational and social worlds. It demands that they accept schooling's definitions and points to the incredibly high rates of academic failure as proof of their inadequacies. By shaming, excluding, devaluing, and alienating Afro-American children, teachers give youngsters a truer sense of where they stand in the social system of the United States. In these acts of inculcation and socialization,

Afro-American children learn that they probably will not be president of the United States, that is, they learn their place in the economic and social pyramid.

Some learn the messages of the racist state schools and lose much of their self-esteem, becoming ashamed of their families and heritage. Other Afro-American children respond to the racist messages of state schools by shutting them out, seeking to reaffirm their identities as competent and worthwhile persons by going back to familial, neighborhood, or nationalist groups. They accentuate the values and world views of their race and try to understand the exact nature of the racism which is arrayed against them. While schooling is teaching such children they are unworthy and incompetent, Afro-American organizations are trying to counteract these teachings and their effects on the social and personality structures of children. Now and then these ideas find their way into parts of the curriculum of an individual school. But these learnings are soon overwhelmed by the other pedagogic demands of state schools, demands focused on test scores, which are racially and culturally biased against Afro-Americans.

IDEOLOGY IN ACTION

Ideology is the way we think about our lives. It is also the way classes struggle for supremacy in the social and economic sectors of society. People seldom reflect upon the assumptions and distortions that dominate much of their thinking. They do not pay much attention to their class position in society, save in a general, commonsense way. Althusser and the structural Marxists separated theory from practice and ideology and language from the ongoing efforts of people to understand why they are alive and what problems are most pressing for them. This led individuals to see social reality as a creation of human consciousness rather than a struggle for power between competing classes. Ideology is a social force in our lives, and despite its distortion of the object world, it contains knowledge that has been developed in praxis. This knowledge is often a common consciousness of groups or classes and forms the basis for understanding the social reality that confronts individuals at work and in school. Because the knowledge gained in this way is necessarily fragmentary, it seldom empowers people. The consciousness of ideologies is the consciousness of dominant and subordinate classes, and those of the dominant classes usually rule the day in state institutions like the schools. If we think of educational systems as autonomous institutions that can be reformed by new and enlightened practices, we think ideologically about such problems. Knowledge begins when we see schooling as part of a totality, as an instrument of the state and the dominant classes in capitalist society. Improving schooling, then, becomes problematic, because training future labor replacements requires an apprenticeship that accepts class-bound forms of material production. An individual's social consciousness begins with these types of reflections and with a movement away from just getting through the school day. When we are able to change our way of thinking about teaching and learning in schools, we change the way they affect us in everyday practice. Ideologies are formed in the ongoing relations between teachers and students, but they are structured on a higher level of authority by bureaucrats who represent the interests of the possessing classes. If teachers and students fail to grasp this feature of their classroom lives, they come to see their relations as autonomous, unrelated phenomena happening to them alone. The personalities that are structured in such arbitrary, authoritarian settings have been discussed earlier in this book. Here we can add that teachers expand their personalities into their classrooms because they are the authority figures and have been given the decisional rights in the classroom situation. They decide everything that is to take place there. Students, on the other hand, tend to draw back from classroom activities as much as possible, forming ideas about themselves that develop from their dependent and subordinate positions in the learning situation. Teachers have ideological explanations for their arbitrary behaviors, for their imposition of cultural arbitraries on children. And youngsters have their own ideological understandings of classroom life and how they can survive there.

Only when teachers and students understand the internal relatedness between the struggles at the point of production in educational and social structures can heightened consciousness begin to appear. Only then can they see how ideologies are formed to cloud these relationships and maintain the social relations in schools and the workplace. Ideological struggles are of secondary importance, but they are important nevertheless. They make it less possible for many to join and participate in unions. They provide a rationale for ideological state apparatuses like the schools, the family, the church, and the media. These, in turn, play a pivotal role in developing a sense of self in students and teachers. They also provide rationales for accepting in an unquestioning way the economic system and social inequalities as they exist in society.

Language is another important instrument of communication and understanding, but it, too, is related to the class structures and struggles that develop in the workplace and schools. The language that a person speaks either empowers him or locates him on a scale of declining power and influence in social life. From Bourdieu we have learned that language and culture are two forms of capital that can be spent in class-bound schools in capitalist society. The way an individual speaks tells a great deal about him, his social class, his ethnic background, and what part of the country he lived in as a child.

In racial politics, as an example, it is possible to study the effects of segregation in schools and society by studying the language individuals use to get across their messages. We can hear how teachers describe Afro-American youth in inner-city schools and neighborhoods. We can observe law enforcement and politicians talk to such youth while ignoring the gang-infested pockets of crime and poverty around them. We can listen to educators complaining about admission policies that enforce affirmative action policies. In classrooms, we can observe teachers sending minority children the message that they are not good enough, that they are slow learners who really shouldn't expect much when they reach adulthood. Finally, we can see how such youth are victimized by stereotypes and their enforced segregation from white youth and society. In these instances, language can be studied as a communication factor in the concrete social experiences of Afro-American youth living in segregated ghettos, studying in schools that have been programmed for failure. This study of language would not be separated from the actual experiences of people suffering from such language usage from one generation to the next. It was when Afro-Americans challenged the separate but equal doctrine in American society that white America began to see it as an injustice. It was when Rosa Parks refused to give up her seat on a bus to a white man, when she refused to go to the back of the bus, that white Americans began to see Afro-Americans as human beings who were suffering deep injustices. Challenges to society and its schools made that generation ashamed and forced an attempt to integrate the educational system for the next few decades. Language changed the way Afro-Americans had always been portrayed in state ideological apparatuses like the family, the schools, the church, and the media. We began to change our ideas about segregated housing and employment patterns. However, when the backlash to these policies set in, language was once again used to constitute Afro-Americans as a distinct group seeking preferential treatment for themselves and their children. Americans then reverted to attitudes and practices that had their beginnings in the racism of the past. Afro-Americans began to question how much independence and power they could gain in such a segregated, racist society. Their needs and the needs of their children were trampled upon by neighborhoods and schools that were unsafe and ineffective, by any standard. As they sought to reassert their humanity, they found themselves characterized repeatedly in hostile stereotypes. Their separation caused them to speak a different language from others in the population, to see things in different ways. Their needs and wants were shunted aside because they lacked sufficient economic and social power, because they were politically isolated. The self-perceptions of their children were damaged by this de facto system of apartheid. Their aspirations were denied and their struggle with the legal and penal systems accelerated. Drugs and crime became daily occurrences in the inner city streets. In ghetto schools, Afro-American students learned they were not smart enough, that they could not expect to go far in the educational system or in the labor market. Their responsibility was to continue to try, no matter how many times they failed. They were to prepare themselves for work on the lower rungs of the occupational ladder, even though no such work was available. No student could find work without an education, they were told. Yet most had older brothers and sisters who had been unable to find any work at all. How did young students learn all this? They heard it from parents or adults in their homes. They listened while older teenagers and youth spoke of their frustrated efforts to find work. They learned from their elders and from teachers who also limited their aspirations, their futures. They were destined for failure in schools and work, much as those who had gone before them.

These lessons of language provide Afro-American youth in ghettos with a reasonably accurate picture of their social and economic position in society. They were learned from kinfolk and neighbors in day-to-day discourse and associations and in their schools. They formed a common cultural stock or heritage that helped youth to understand, in a limited way, what was happening to them in their lives. It taught them about themselves and about accepting, without too much thought, their class position and the economic and social system in which they lived.

THE QUESTION OF FREE WILL

Structural theorists, as we have seen, believe that the work of ideology, and ideological state apparatuses like the family and schools produce a linguistic definition of individuals that they then come to recognize as themselves. The individual has no free will. He cannot understand his social conditions or change them. But Marx was explicit in his call to arms. Implicitly, this call must be to individuals who are subjects capable of understanding and changing their social conditions. The teacher and student live their lives in the classroom as persons who can determine what is happening to them. Many of the outcomes of their experiences together are other than either of them would wish or intend, leading us to think again about the Althusserian idea that they are make-believe subjects without consciousness or free will. We have discussed in chapter 4 some of the strengths and problems associated with these ideas. If there is any possibility of using the schools in more constructive and humane ways, then teachers, students, and parents will have to be seen as real persons who can effectuate some small measure of change. This approach helps to maintain some relationship between theory and the social reality of the perceived world. Conscious actions by individuals have changed the political conditions in ways that seem to be beyond mere determinism. Marx saw the class struggle as the motor of human history. Dominant and subordinate classes struggled with one another for scarce resources or commodities, for primacy and power. These class relations were determined by the social relations that developed in the production processes of material wealth, as discussed in chapter 5. In modern times, the struggle has been between labor and those who own and control the means of production.

Marx's theories implied a subject who was part of a social class during a specific period in human history. He was at the center of the class struggle, not just an object effected by it. For Marx, ideology had its primary impetus in the class struggle. From the moment an individual is born, he is influenced by this struggle between the classes. In the family and schools, the language and culture of class are learned and passed on from one generation to the next. These two agencies are not separate and apart from other social formations in society. They are entwined with them and effected by social, political, and economic institutions. The individual acquires a class identity before birth, before schooling begins, before his entrance into the labor market. The family is not separate from the times in which it lives. It is not an autonomous agency. It is defined by its relationship to the dominant mode of production. This definition determines where it will reside, what schools it will attend, what work it will be able to get, and so on. The struggle between working people and those who control their instruments of labor is present in the structures that come to dominate in the families themselves. How many children will a family have? How stable will marriages be? How extended will family life become? Will old people live with their families, or will they be sent to old-age homes? When an individual is born, he or she is given a class identity regardless of sex or color. However, these last two categories change fundamentally the way he or she is treated and the way the world is experienced within class boundaries. Marx's worker was asexual, neither man nor woman. The worker was exploited because the surplus value created by his or her labor was expropriated by capitalists for their own advantage. But with the proletarianization of the female population in recent times, sexual differences have become much more important.

The family, the schools and the state appear to be semiautonomous social formations, but they are deeply interrelated to the economic sector of society. They are ideological forms or state apparatuses that have been created by the social relations individuals enter into when they begin to produce wealth. They are part of the productive forces and not separate and apart from them. The class struggle occurs because of the different interests and positions that individuals and families have in the social pyramid, which affect the ways in which children are socialized and taught in state schools.

These ideas can help us to study the meanings and effects of pedagogic action in schools. In schools, as in all human endeavors, an unconscious process will form a part of the meaning of all communications, thus providing us with layers of understanding. But to see educational production as the dissemination of the dominant culture's views and understandings of contemporary life is to affirm the importance of conflict and antagonism between the haves and have-nots of society. Students are not empty shells that can be filled up with knowledge. The Battle of Bunker Hill cannot hold much interest for inner-city minority students unless it is also related to the contributions of their forefathers. The study of such curriculum places certain children outside and apart from the heritages they must learn about, even as they become more ignorant of their own heritage. A study of these messages and their hidden intentions would be a good first step toward transforming schooling into an educational experience.

Probably no where else has the anticommunist, anti-union hysteria been so systematically promulgated as in the state schools of the United States. With communism, the method has been to pass on attitudes that preceded the Palmer Raids of the 1920s, exposing such systems as inherently evil and destructive of everything decent people hold dear. In the case of unionism, there has been a benign neglect, as though the coming together of tens of million of Americans at different times in our history was of little importance or concern to students in state schools. Combined with the virulent anti-unionism of the media, the total effect has been one in which workers of all sorts have developed anti-union biases and stereotypes that have weakened the working conditions of all Americans. The defense of American society against the communists required the efforts of state schools and universities as well as all of the other institutions in society. The subject was distorted by patriotic attitudes and teaching, which were disposed to denigrate the implications of these other forms of social organization. Again and again there have been inquisitions wherein books have been removed from shelves because they taught materials that were too liberal or taught scientific theories that disagreed with the beliefs of parents and community members.

Finally, state schools reflect the attitudes and culture of bourgeois society. They tend toward greater impersonality and amorality, reflecting the materialistic biases of capitalist economics. They teach an easy acceptance of competition and militarism, justifying both as essential to maintaining the wealth and security of the nation. Of course schooling pays lip service to democracy in much the same way as capitalists do; but in their practices they are antidemocratic and authoritarian, as are the structures workers encounter in the workplace.

The ideology that state apparatuses transmit teach only the formal organization of democracy and its limitations in times of crisis. Democracies are ruled by the people, and the masses are unschooled or too ignorant to govern wisely. Legislative branches of government often cannot free themselves from the financial control exerted by capitalists, and democracies degenerate into plutocracies in which the rich rule. Democracy is opposed to capitalism. The resources of a nation are under the control of a few in the latter system, while in the former the people could be expected to use resources for the benefit of the many. Democratic solutions to social and economic problems would satisfy few people because of the compromises they would demand. When ruling classes of capitalists are added to this equation, the balance of power tips completely in favor of the rich and powerful. Again and again Americans are told there is no money for improving state schools or social services, but hundreds of billions are spent to bail out banks or equip huge peacetime armies with devastating weapons of modern warfare.

Marx studied the workplace in the capitalism of his day, noting the discrepancy of power between the worker who comes to the hiring hall with hat in hand and the capitalist who sits full of self-assurance and power at his desk waiting to see whom he wishes to employ. The disparity of power in the economic sector carries into every other area of social life, defining the class positions of individuals in society. Once the worker has been hired, he finds himself in the most autocratic and dictatorial of surroundings. The boss makes it clear that *he* is the boss and that the worker is to do what he is told. The boss decides where the worker will work, how he will do the work, how long he will work each day, and how much he will be paid for his labor. The reader may see that this situation is the one that state schooling has prepared individual students to accept in their adulthood. The transition from antidemocratic school settings to workplaces takes place without too much difficulty.

It was in the workplace that Marx turned for the essential relationships in society. Here the inequalities between workers and capital could be studied and the rights of each carefully documented. The freedom of capitalists to hire and fire were contrasted with the indentured nature of the workers' experience; the equality between men of capital, at least in so far as their legal rights were concerned, was contrasted with the lesser status and economic condition of workers; and finally, the right to own property was seen as one that applied to only a select few in society.

Many of these truths apply to schools, where students are taught that freedom, equality, and the right to own property are the inalienable rights of Americans. Yet many of the educational practices of educational systems have little to do with any of these values. This is because they are in contradiction to the dominant cultural arbitrary Bourdieu spoke of in his theories of schooling. Capitalists and educators, as mentioned earlier, permit little or no freedom for their workers or students, insisting that the body of the employee or pupil be rigidly controlled during the work or schooling experience. Equality is paid lip service in schools, where the teacher dominates and children simply listen and respond when spoken to. And finally, students own none of the means of educational production in state schools, and they have no opportunity to gain such ownership. They are permitted to work in classrooms when schools are opened, not when they feel an urge to study some subject with which they are concerned. The fact that educational production is sexist may be obscured for many because of the large number of female teachers in elementary and secondary schools. But these persons work in a state ideological apparatus that espouses a militaristic and patriarchal philosophy, which they themselves have internalized over a long period of schooling. Yet consciousness sometimes comes into play in the experiences of some of these women (and men) and causes them to react in ways that contradict dominant, sexist ideologies. They begin to look for ways to "make their classrooms more human," "more child-oriented," and so on. Marxism has always sought vindication for its concepts in the experiences of people living together in capitalist society. Eliminating experience entirely, as Althusser has done, deprives individuals of any opportunity to develop knowledge outside that of the dominant ideology. They cannot act as effective political agents in the workplace or school. Workers cannot become conscious of their true conditions of existence; they cannot act as subjects who force a change in the way things are produced and distributed in modern society.

Althusser's divorce of social theory from reality is necessarily incomplete in spite of its brilliant insights into language and culture. In schooling, the dominant ideology of the state and capitalist classes suppress and distort educational learnings that run counter to their own interests. This omission of the experiences and values of millions of teachers and students may be difficult to identify or explain, but their effects are obvious: educational knowledge is produced in ways that sort out minorities, the working classes, women, and so on. The point may be made by the following example. Hispanic failure in schools is usually represented in ideological stereotypes, considering their difficulties as one of culture, class, and language. The Hispanic family is seen as teaching children a way of living that is in conflict with the white, Anglo-Saxon culture of schools in the United States. The mythical ideas about Hispanics include another component: even though some of them succeed in schools, they are not capable or intelligent enough to do very well in academic affairs. These ideas have persisted in spite of research showing that many Hispanics have done well in schools and that their high rates of failure can be explained by continuing immigration and their impoverished conditions in inner cities. The ideological explanations also contain explanations that point to the language problems of students, without also citing the schools' inability to teach Hispanic children how to read, speak, and write English. Blame is always placed on the children or their families, with educational systems using a client-culpability theory to explain their failure to educate youngsters effectively. School books and other materials are usually full of the experiences and cultural outlook of the majority population, and Hispanic children are taught at an early age that their family, language, and heritage are not the same as the ones being portrayed as desirable in state schools. The Hispanic experience in American history is conspicuously missing from texts and from the knowledge or consciousness of teachers. It is discouraging to learn how many teachers of Hispanic children know little or no Spanish and even less about the rich heritage these children could learn about in their classrooms. Of course, attempts to rectify these situations, which are suggested from time to time, lose out to the inevitable budget cuts and the lack of personnel truly committed to making such programs work. Thus the failure rates reported by schools in Southern California and Texas hovered around the 40 percent level as late as 1989.

A sociocultural theory of schooling that seeks to overturn such ideological effects needs to be grounded in the individual's ability to heighten his or her consciousness of schooling experiences. The importance of ideological conflict is a very real one in educational systems. It is a conflict over who will decide how the experiences of working-class and middle-class people are to be described and preserved in the valid knowledge passed on by schooling. It also reflects the demands of ethnic and racial minorities that they cease to be invisible persons with little or no culture and history worthy of study. Finally, it is an insistence that the dominant ideologies make room for the aspirations of different groups and classes and society, even if capitalist society cannot make room for them. Finally, it symbolizes the struggle to change the social relations of educational and economic production so that more democratic forms of government and schooling can come into being. This is why the schools are such an important location of the class struggle in modern society. Here, and here alone, the masses of children come together to receive instruction and inculcation that will determine the future of modern societies.

In schooling, ideas and ideologies develop out of lived experiences in classrooms and communities. Later, they may develop into full-blown theories. With the demand for inculcation in state schools, the division between teachers and students becomes crystalized in social forms that are the product of understandings that have their beginnings in the practical activities of schooling in capitalist systems. The interests of teachers and students differ, as do the interest of students from different classes in society. These differences are part of the ideological struggle that occurs in classrooms, but they occur in a context of other ideologies that are socially supportive of the very symbolic violence being committed against children in state schools. This is because, as Bourdieu taught us, they misrecognize their situations, taking the ideology of schooling for its essence. Ideas become parts of ideologies when they distort reality for teachers and students in the interests of dominant classes that are structuring classroom activities from outside the classroom. As the ideas become part of the common cultural heritage, or arbitrary habitus, they appear as separate and apart from the classes they were meant to benefit. They become accepted explanations of the work being done between teachers and students. In this sense, Althusser's notions of the individual as object incapable of understanding his position in society seems pertinent. But struggle implies subjectivity, as we have stated. It also implies that schooling needs to be understood within the context of the social relations of production in operation at different times and places. It is not necessary to attach economic reasons to every practice in the production of educational knowledge in state schools, as some have done. Yet economic forces are powerful agencies in the ideological conflict that takes place in schools.

Conceptualizing educational knowledge as production removes it from the arena of reflection and reintroduces it as a social relation that has internal-relatedness to other sectors in society, especially the economic. Educational production is not a matter for reflection and theoretical discourse in an autonomous institution. It is a concrete occupational activity, and its product, which takes many years to turn out, has a real effect on the economy and social life of the system. Of course, thinking or reflection can be thought of as a form of labor, one which is steeped in ideas and language. This leads to an ideological effect that has its own material basis in fact, that is, in the ideas of the dominant classes in society. Teachers do have the materials of production, or the brains of children who need to be socialized and instructed. And they do transform these individuals over time into persons who have their places in the economic and social activities of the nation. Educational production should be studied in terms of the relations of production that are ascendant in a particular time and place and the practices that develop to maintain and reproduce those relations. The social relations of educational production are deeply influenced by capital, transforming children into saleable commodities, that is, into wage earners. As such, schooling plays an important role in the ongoing life of the social system. Schools and families are important centers of ideological production. They exist outside the marketplace, but the conditions of their existence are deeply affected by social and economic institutions in society.

Unlike commodities in the economic arena, educational production does not have use and surplus value that can be readily exploited. The amount of labor required to produce future wage earners cannot be understood in these economic terms. The surplus value is too far in the future to be the reason for the labor expended on children in their families and schools. Whatever surplus value is produced will not be evident until children have finished with schooling and entered into the labor market.

7

Separating Theory from Practice: A Scholastic Question

Marx concerned himself with a concrete and observable problem: the "hiding" working men experienced when they sold their labor. The unequal relationship between workers and capitalists became the centerpiece of his mature work, the core from which all later abstractions followed. Marxist and sociocultural studies of schooling have moved away from these methods, preferring coherence-based, logical theories that separate ideas from classroom realities. Teachers struggle with themselves, their students, and the curriculum they teach. They may not recognize the symbolic violence inherent in their actions, but that does not mean they are incapable of such recognition. They may not see how their labor contributes to the consolidation of class interests and structures, but they could come to grasp these aspects of their work. Often, they may not be conscious of the way current practices oppress minority and poor children but, again, they are capable of such awareness. The failure of teachers to see what they are doing to students does not mean they are misrecognizing the situation, either. Rather they may be focusing on the social solidarity-producing aspects of their work, using these effects to condone or legitimize their impositional behaviors. These aspects of schooling are ideological, but no less real than other forms of ideas and communications. If we accept structural Marxist theories, we choose abstraction over everyday interactions in schools and society. Marx's manifesto now becomes absurd, as it then is addressed not to subjects who think and act, but to objects who are merely linguistic constructs. The struggle of minority children in American schools is considered too empirical, too affected by ideology to provide us with the theoretical insights. The internationalization of the labor market is also disconnected from such theories, as is the schooling which prepares students to be replacement workers. The failure of workers, teachers, students, and parents to understand their positions in capitalist society has led some to seek answers in more abstract conceptualizations. Rather than criticize their previous work as being too one-sided, too obsessed with conflict, exploitation, and oppression, these structural Marxists have sought to explain things by using misrecognition concepts similar to the false consciousness of older theories. Instead of seeing the social-solidarity aspects of ideological structures they choose to see only the distorting propensities of ideological thought. The desire of minorities to assimilate into the American culture and workplace is paid scant attention, and their oppression is described without resorting to empirical evidence. To the extent that minorities want a bigger piece of the capitalist pie, they are dismissed as dupes of the system and its ideological effects.

That is not meant to cast aside Althusser's work, nor to ignore his help in breaking with economistic theories of class struggle. The intellectual work of Bourdieu, Balibar, and Lacan have helped us to focus on inculcation and the construction of the individual's identity in mass society. But like blind men touching an elephant, they have tended to ignore that which is outside the Marxist tradition: the genuine, socially binding effects of family and educational experiences, even as these constrain and delimit the life possibilities of children. Even when distortions of such experiences are understood, individuals still cling to ideological understandings of themselves, their class position, and their cultural heritages. Theoretical work cannot be based solely on empiricism or rationalism, and it cannot divorce itself from political and social practice. Theories that separate themselves as production still need to enunciate what connections they have to the subject matter they address. The struggle and critical issues of our period need to be closely integrated into theoretical formulations, not made into a separate practice unavailable to workers, the poor, and minorities.

The work of structural Marxists utilizes a rationalist perspective or theory of knowledge. In it, ideology and knowledge are juxtaposed to one another, even as they admit that the former is constructed of statements and ideas that have proven their worth to people in their daily experiences. But Marx's ideas about the relations between theory and practice are related to Hegelian thought and integrate these two forms of knowledge. Marx viewed the question of human objectivity as a practical question, not a theoretical one. Human beings must prove the truth or falsity of their thought in everyday interaction with the physical and social world. Theory isolated from practice is an intellectual exercise of the academic community, a "purely scholastic question." Marxism was not conceived of as a philosophy. Indeed, Marx was antagonistic toward philosophy and chose to do his work in political economy. He opted for the concrete relations between workers and capitalists as his starting point, and through a method of successive approximations he developed his theories into explanations of class conflict in human history and society.

Those who wish to think about schooling in modern society must pay attention to the history and practice of this ideological apparatus. Theoretical production exists, but contrary to Althusser's work, its language, ideas, and understandings are formed in praxis, in actual classroom experiences. Even when theorists claim a separation from reality, they create an artificial discourse by refusing to recognize their assumptions and ideological biases. The idea of classroom interaction cannot exist outside an individual's stream of consciousness, as structural Marxists have emphasized. It is a reflective, ideological construct, but it can only be demystified when it is related to the reality it seeks to understand. Likewise the struggle for dominance in the classroom (and workplace) can be seen by participants and observers alike. But its existence comes to the fore only when the individual is no longer participating or observing, when he or she reflects upon what has been experienced. Only then can it be said that educational production has occurred. Of course, such classroom observances can be understood in many ways, and the theoretician needs to choose how to conceptualize them. These choices will be determined, in part, by the political and ideological systems that he or she supports. Marx believed that philosophical theories were little more than apologies for political attitudes, owing their influence to the economic and social realities of a particular time and place in history.

Children in inner-city schools come to their classrooms with commonsense understandings of what they can expect once the school day begins. These grow out of religious, racial, moral, and familial understandings and ideas that have been taught to them. Children and teachers carry these ideological explanations with them as they start their classroom work together. These orientations can be seen as "philosophies" that reflect the views of competing classes, races, and ethnic groups. Children may come expecting humiliation and failure as their daily fare, as their parents and older siblings did before them. Or they may develop elaborate moral philosophies to justify and explain the impositional behavior of teachers and the symbolic violence that accompanies pedagogic action.

So we must ask once again, what can we expect from sociocultural theories of schooling today? Should theoretical insights be put to the test of science? Can such knowledge improve educational practice? Or is it foolish to assume that pedagogic action could ever be changed while schooling remains tied to the workplace in capitalist society?

From Schutz we have learned that there is a difference between the "in order to" mode of thinking that people use to get through daily experiences together and the "because" mode they use once they begin to reflect on those experiences. Individuals are capable of such reflective actions, of applying a critical faculty to their experiences at home, in school, and in the workplace. After the individual is transformed into the social person through language, she moves on to new levels of growth and development. Much of what she believes comes to her from her parents and family, and she usually accepts these values, ideas, and beliefs without question. Indeed, she is often unaware that she is receiving these ideological effects through osmosis. For her acceptance of them, she receives social approval from individuals who are important to her and to her psychological health and well-being. But as she matures, her experiences make her aware of other ideas and cultural perspectives. Now and then, she begins to think critically about her personal philosophy and way of understanding the world. She comes now to the crossroads that the German philosopher Nietzsche spoke of: she can continue to believe and accept the ideas of her family and kinfolk, her church, and her schoolteachers, or she can place these ideas in doubt. Believing carries with it an acceptance by significant others. It leads to peace of soul and happiness. Doubting, on the other hand, leads to uncertainty and loneliness and rejection by those who were closest to the individual in her infancy and childhood.

In this philosophy the individual is obviously a subject, a subject who can criticize and doubt. She has a consciousness that can grasp relationships in schools and the workplace, even though this consciousness is usually dormant and controlled by unconscious forces seemingly beyond her control. So, as an example, learning in an inner city elementary school in a large city, a child might not think much about her future and the ways success in schooling might help her in later life. This could be because her mother never went past second grade and her father was no longer living with them. She may be able to get some idea of her class position in school and society, but more likely she will simply accept the ideas and aspirations of her working mother. When she questions the way teachers discipline her, her mother may slap her face and insist that she obey everything the teacher tells her to do.

Her consciousness may be raised, however, by her fear and dislike of teachers and classroom routines. Talking to friends, she may come to see that her feelings were shared by many others who were also attending this inner city school. She might begin to think about what she was learning in class and why she found it so boring and unrelated to her life. She might also think about the many children who failed in their schoolwork, making them feel incompetent and unworthy of consideration or respect. If she was lucky enough to find someone to talk to, she could enter the reflective mode and begin to cast a critical eye on her learning experiences. She could make herself a more conscious person, breaking out of the unconscious motivations that control so much of her life at home and in school. She could become aware of the ways in which schooling in her inner city classrooms was influencing her own feelings of self-worth and the way she thought about her family and friends. These insights could help her to move from problems in the classroom to other problems that have to do with her future in higher education and the labor market. This kind of awareness might not happen for many years, but when it did happen, it could have a cumulative effect. One question would lead to the next, and she would get a better idea about how her family's socioeconomic standing in society limited her horizons in the social and economic world.

The experience of Afro-Americans since the 1960s seems to indicate such a conscious-raising experience. The civil rights movement forced segregated American institutions to look again at their racist practices, resulting in attempts to assure the vote to Afro-Americans and desegregate the schools. The racial consciousness of these years sprang from the people themselves. They decided not to participate in segregated practices; they challenged society to live up to its stated ideals. These challenges had their beginnings in the awareness of Afro-Americans that discriminatory practices were un-American and could be changed through disciplined, nonviolent protests. This is not to say that ideas, even those which espouse democracy and human equality, will not suffer as they are transformed from words and ideas to reality. Afro-Americans were able to confront many people with the variance between what they professed and what they actually did in their daily lives. They were also able to make it plain to white Americans that segregation and discrimination, even in de facto forms, was both unethical and unconstitutional and needed to end. Of course segregation is still with us today, and racism permeates our schools and economic and social institutions. In this sense, the conscious-raising of the 1960s can be seen as a deception, an ideological movement that failed to understand that capitalist America could not and would not stop the oppression of Afro-Americans in response to ethical and legal arguments. The schools and workplace were and are part of an oppressive system, which cannot be changed with words or ideas. Yet the fact that so many millions joined together to fight for these egalitarian ideas cannot be ignored or cast aside. Their actions mean that, even though the thought of the people is distorted by ideology, they are capable of understanding, in an approximate way, elements of their true position in the capitalist system.

The demand for submission in classrooms and workshops shapes the personality and consciousness of individuals. So does the dependent, powerless role that individuals are forced to play in these institutions. The student or worker cannot play out the role of the conscious or active person, because their role has been otherwise defined. It is known that students and teachers have their own view of what is happening between them, even though the students' views are seldom expressed. Likewise the workers may appear to be automatons in the workshop, because their labor contracts demand that they perform the same simple operations again and again during the work day. Students rarely have an opportunity to come together to talk about their situations, but workers have formed unions in an attempt to protect themselves from the arbitrariness they experience in the workplace. Their ideas are shaped from experiences on the job and from the understandings they develop about the conflict between workers and employers. These ideas are transferred to language and shared in ways that allow for concerted actions in the social arena, even as they distort the realities they seek to describe. Thus approximate knowledge of social reality, sufficient to allow for concerted effort, is possible and deserves some place in theoretical efforts to understand schooling and the workplace. Theory divorced from the daily lives of people, from their social, economic, and political struggles, is of interest only to savants who live and work in distant ivory towers.

A final example shows the teachers' ability to act consciously in their struggle for better working conditions and wages in the New York City schools in the late 1950s and 1960s. Teachers had been intimidated and fragmented by authorities after honor picketing their schools and holding union meetings on "school grounds." They were frustrated, angry, and unaware of the history of the profession in New York's schools. They joined in a citywide strike, picketing schools and insisting upon better conditions for themselves and the children they served. This developed into a strike over teachers' rights to organize and to have more of a say in what they did once they were in the school building. As far as most teachers could see, these problems were caused by reactionary, short-sighted politicians and educators and a lack of respect for schoolteachers. They refused to subsidize public education by accepting the traditionally low wages paid by city and state officials. This caused them to come together as a group in spite of their antipathy toward unions and one another. The ideological demands of fairness and equity were coupled with others for smaller class sizes, more educational materials and texts, and special schools for children who were failing in regular classrooms. On the day of the strike, there was confusion, with twenty thousand teachers showing up for work and an equal number walking picket lines. Many felt that striking was wrong and hurt children; others pointed to the fact that it was against the law for teachers to strike in the state, saying that strikers should be fired and thrown in jail! Many of the strikers, on the other hand, felt things could not go on as they had in the past. They needed and deserved a living wage; their students deserved smaller classes, more individual attention, new ways of teaching and learning, and new and more relevant materials. Many called those who were working "scabs" and felt they were too cowardly to take action on their own behalf and on behalf of their children. These strikers had set themselves in opposition to the state, the city, the board, and school administrators. They believed that deep changes were needed in the structure and practices of public schools. Their feelings were strengthened by the angry attitudes of administrators, who threatened them with disciplinary actions and firings if they joined the union, participated in the strike, or met together to discuss these matters. The struggle was over the old and the new, over who would ultimately control and operate the schools. This struggle was part of a series of struggles that had started in the past, not something that suddenly appeared on the horizon. Only now teachers were forced into consciousness as younger members, who had benefited from the G.I. Bill programs after World War II, entered the profession. Many of these newcomers were men and women who had to support families on their meager salaries.

The changing relationships between teachers and administrators were a result of the heightened consciousness of teachers, who came together to change the social and educational conditions in their cities' schools. They were a consequence of historical experiences of teachers, who had often faced their employers disunited and uncertain of their economic and educational needs and demands. Many teachers had come to accept a subservient position in schools once they were outside their classrooms, and these relationships and attitudes had a long and dishonorable history.

This strike happened after World War II, when a large number of atypical college graduates entered the teaching profession. They forced a change of attitude and orientation among teachers, insisting on new approaches to the way schools were organized. Sociocultural theories of schooling will have to make sense of these historical events and the ways they changed teaching and learning in inner-city schools. Teachers found that the work of teaching no longer gave them a sense of satisfaction and identity they could accept. Many of these teachers had outside lives that were much more important to them than their schoolwork. It was after school that they could be individuals with worth and value, that they could participate in the new counterculture just beginning to take hold in the United States.

It has been through these kind of actions that schooling's limitations and failures had been discussed in recent years. Theories that are separate and apart from the realities of classroom life are simply not adequate. Theory isn't something that is separate and apart from the social, economic, and political realities of life. It comes into consciousness because it has affinities with institutional needs in a particular time and place, as the German sociologist Max Weber showed. Sociocultural theories of schooling should not develop outside the experiences and consciousness of teachers and students. Rather, they should use methods of successive approximations to develop hypotheses and glosses that stem from the essential relationship of the learning experience, that of the teacher and student. From this relationship other variables can be systematically added to create a clearer picture of the conflicts and questions that are important to people who are going through the inculcation and symbolic violence of classroom interactions. It is in this comparison of theoretical concepts to ongoing interactions in the world that sociocultural theories of schooling and society can become most meaningful. It is in the use of history, with all its problems, that theory can be given a longitudinal feature that places it in its proper context.

RECREATING CLASS STRUCTURES IN SCHOOLS AND SOCIETY

Katznelson and Weir and Gintis and Bowles seek to show how class structures in American society were recreated in the nation's schools.[1,2] Their starting point is schooling in the nineteenth and early twentieth centuries, when the educational system became an important agency of capitalism. Both recognize that schools had specific functions. Both find a definitive relationship between capitalist methods of production and the establishment of public schools. Taking at face value the words and ideological pronouncements of common school adherents, they declare that the new modes of production needed educational reform and expansion to prepare a literate and capable working class and citizenry. A structural correspondence is said to exist between the social relations found in educational practice and those of the workplace. Classrooms are thus seen as parodies of workshops, with teachers playing the capitalists' role and students that of the workers. Both sets of authors recognize schooling as the agency responsible for reproducing the class structures in schools and society. This was because capitalism had no other way to prepare the next generation to receive and accept the conditions of the workplace.

Both sets of authors agree that the working class supported public schools for their own purposes, but Katznelson and Weir ask further: Why was this demand of workers achieved while so many others were not? Their answer is that working people achieved their demands only when they were part of a broad political coalition. Gintis and Bowles state that schools produced workers, but Katznelson and Weir chide them for not answering how this was done. No mention is made of ideology or its part in selling the different classes on the establishment of schooling in the United States. No mention is made of language and culture and the way these distorted the consciousness of workers in the emerging industrial system. The authors, seemingly unaware of pedagogical action as symbolic violence, willingly quote the words and ideas of persons who lived in the past as though such citations constituted reliable evidence. But the words of individuals who lived in the past were uttered after the fact or before they were aware of what schooling would actually be like for immigrant and working-poor children. The transformation of social demands for schooling into language transformed social reality in significant ways, but this is not mentioned by these authors. Yet the demand for common schooling was made in language, causing the ideological perspectives of working-class and dominant-class individuals to come into play and further distorting reality.

Katznelson and Weir begin their work by reviewing the separation that took place when home industries were replaced by more advanced forms of industrial production. Workers were forced to leave their households to perform work, and separate districts were established for residential and business locations. One consequence: men and women of similar status, race, class, and ethnicity began to congregate in increasingly homogeneous neighborhoods. The schools established by local governments adopted neighborhood concepts as a matter of course, accepting the idea that schools should be as near as possible to the homes of children. A consequence of these policies was race and class segregation, two practices that undermined education's stated goals of assimilation and social equality.

Both sets of authors agree that the establishment of common schools was characterized by class struggles and an adaption to the needs of capitalist production. These shaped the educational system. Shifts in the locus and mode of production forced schooling to assume the role of the trainer, preparing youth to be laborers capable of doing routine work and maintaining a subordinate demeanor. Both describe class attitudes toward schooling, but do so by referring to the ideological pronouncements of participants. In this they seem guilty of accepting appearance for essence, although they do mention that the reality of pedagogic training was quite different from what it promised. As their work is essentially historical, they pounce on evidences that the working classes accepted, with few reservations, the new state schools.

Issues of immigration and nativism did present issues of contention and struggle, as did the pockets of poverty that arose in urban centers. What did the public expect from their common schools? They expected a literate and virtuous citizenry capable of integrating themselves into the workplace and republic. There was general agreement on the objectives of common schools and the processes they should employ in classrooms, save for Roman Catholics. Both sets of authors seem to press for a direct relationship between capitalism and schooling's practices, preferring a functional approach. Katznelson and Weir focus on state-building, citizenship, and federalism as a framework for broadening their understanding of how schooling developed in capitalist America. Changes in the amount of time spent in schools surged with growth in the economy. Schools were given the task of maintaining the social and economic order by reproducing the labor force from one generation to the next. Yet these arguments depend too heavily on historical proofs, proofs that are seldom analyzed for their ideological effects. The authors acknowledge a variance between what is said and done in schools, but this is never made the subject of their studies.

Returning to the work processes, spatial dislocations destroyed the family economic unit of an earlier age. Urban centers were divided in ways that ripped apart old patterns of kinship and social control. Work was separated from residences, and more families came to be female dominated, when both parents were not working outside the home. The government sought to respond in three ways: first, they attempted to regulate where work could be performed, how many workers could work in a particular location, and so on; second, they used their right of franchise to involve workers and their leaders in the social order in ways that least threatened to disrupt the social order and marketplace; and lastly, they developed new political relationships with residential areas, placing schools within the domain of local government. The traditional relationships of the gemeinschaft were replaced by social controls that relied upon public authority and policing. The class struggle between workers and employers was now displaced by a struggle within the politics of the state, where all supposedly met as free and equal citizens. The authors give scant attention to Marx's work on plutocracy or to Lenin's analysis showing that equality was a sham when a few held the wealth and power over the many. Schooling became generally accepted during this period, with ethnic, racial, and religious loyalties blurring class interests. The federal government preoccupied itself with legitimacy and authority at home and abroad, concerning itself with economic problems and the development of overseas markets. Problems of law and order were left to local governments to solve. It was during this period of massive immigration and increasing urban poverty that common schools were funded by local governments during the latter half of the nineteenth century. They were agencies for incorporating youth into the social order, for assuring respect for authority and property. Schooling's functions were expressed in ideological terms of republicanism, freedom, and economic opportunity. Connections were made between these virtues and stability at home and in the workplace. They were based on a supposed belief in the wisdom of the people, on their capacity to decide together the best course of action for themselves and the nation. Common schools were to educate each generation so that the transmission of the nation's institutions would survive unimpaired. These goals were needed, not only for public safety and industrial peace, but for the happiness of the individual citizen. This kind of discourse did much to blur the class interests and concerns of working people, appealing to their identities as citizens in a democratic society.

Still, both sets of authors were able to see the founding of state schools as a process of inculcation and an important site of the class struggle. Historical voting patterns of working-class electorates were cited as proof of the importance working people ascribed to schooling, but the schools themselves are inadequately discussed. Working people believed, wrongly as it seems, that schooling would break the monopoly of education and control that the dominant classes held.

These writers appear to be guilty of empiricism, relying too heavily on the words and texts of participants from the past. They assume that Marx's theories of historical materialism have direct empirical referents that can be used to show causal relations between practices in differing social, economic, and political institutions. They tend to humanize historical experiences, ignoring their assumptions of social order and continuous progress in human affairs. Collective meaning and rational choices are assigned to immigrant and poor people who probably never thought deeply about common schooling or any other issue of their day. They were busy learning a new and difficult language and trying to survive in an economic jungle. Their interests probably did encourage them to support common schools for all, even as some of them must have known that the schools of the rich and powerful would be significantly different from those their children attended. The history and internal development of educational institutions are ignored by the writers, as though they had no part in creating the social relations of educational production in precapitalist and capitalist societies. In both instances, schooling, when it existed, functioned to maintain the status quo.

In these American studies, common schools are seen as emerging from the demands of an industrial, capitalist society. They are an evolutionary process, a logic of social order and progress that forms the hidden assumptions of both groups of authors. Finally, the basic questions about how schools train workers is asked but never seriously addressed. The problematic of these writers is too limited, focusing as it does on a correspondence between the social relations of the workplace and schools. The data is obviously ideological, and the authors treat it in this way without thinking too much about it. But they never examine the ideologies of working and dominant classes as modes of thinking that distorted class positions and understandings about common schools.

The failure to analyze sufficiently the ideological struggle that accompanied the establishment of common schools forces these writers to remain on a historical, economic level of analysis. Working people misrecognized their social and political positions in the republic and their power to influence or control schooling even when it was situated in their neighborhoods. Their consciousness was a false one because they accepted the apparent differences in their working and social identities as real ones. On the job they might be wage slaves who were weak, dependent, and subordinate to others, but at home they were free men. Knowledge was power, then as now, and these immigrant and working poor did not know how government operated or the ways in which wealth corrupted republican institutions. Social consciousness and class ideologies were probably involved in the political and social practices that developed inside classrooms during this period in American history. Changes in schooling represented changes in the power of the American business classes and new needs for a literate and skilled work force. But during this very period, work was becoming more rationalized and simple, the assembly line was becoming more widespread, and bureaucracy was consolidating itself in every arena of American life. This would indicate that, aside from speaking English, there was little schooling could do for the apprentice workers who were passing through their classrooms. And even here, much of the language was learned elsewhere, as the failure rates of schools from 1890 to the present indicate. As for skills, most of the work required precious little of them, with machinery doing more and more of the actual production of commodities.

The formation of working-class personality was completed in the family, the church, and the schools, where the lessons of subordinacy and dependence were brought home on a daily basis. Working-class support for common schools was based on ideological understandings of these state institutions. They thought of them as places where their children would learn what they needed to know to get ahead in society. Instead, they learned how to be the deferential and dependent worker who never thought much about the economic system that was grinding him and his family down. Most working-class children failed to complete elementary school; and when the high schools were first formed, only 6 or 7 percent of youngsters graduated from them. Working-class support for common schools was based on ideological effects and on a desire to improve conditions in the marketplace. It was based on a hope that the children of the immigrant and working poor would learn enough in these schools to break the cycle of poverty that existed in the urban centers of the United States.

For example, for a boy from an average poor or immigrant family in common schools, it would only be normal to strive for good grades and a promotion to a higher grade. He needs to prove himself as bright or brighter than his classmates, thus learning a cardinal ethic of capitalist economics: competition. This boy may feel uneasy in his class because he cannot speak English well. He may also be uncomfortable sitting all day at attention or being subjected to corporal punishment. He talks in a way that sounds funny to the teacher and other students, and he feels slightly ashamed of his family and where they are forced to live. He finds also that he is ashamed to ask others for help and has few friends. His grades are not as good as he hoped they would be. Much later this boy might be able to make sense of these experiences and the feelings of incompetency and unworthiness they caused him. He might even come to see his schooling experiences as a class problem. His awareness that he was an immigrant kid from Eastern Europe and from a poor, working-class family could clarify some things that happened to him in his classrooms. The language used there was foreign to him and to the other members of his family. The culture that was taught was also one that had little to do with his own background and experiences at home. These insights wouldn't change what was happening to him at a later stage in his schooling career, but they would give him an opportunity to expand his consciousness and to understand exactly what kind of training he was being given. It would help him grasp the attitudes of his teachers and the methods they use to instruct him. He might even come to understand why he was made to feel so insignificant and stupid. This would be more than merely learning his place as a working-class boy from immigrant parents. Those lessons were learned at home and in the streets when he tried to play with other boys who had been assimilated earlier. As he expands his understanding of the dominant classes that are dictating what happens in schools, this boy may become more conscious of his own class position and the ways in which such differences determine the pedagogy, curriculum, and evaluation methods he experiences in schools. He may come to see how class differences are reproduced in classrooms and schools. He may see how supposedly fair competition is not fair at all, because it hides the true class character of the language and culture all children must master. If he is able to do all this, it will not be with any help from his teachers or classroom lessons. These were meant to insure that he never think about the class character of his school or the economic system within which he lived.

EDUCATIONAL PRODUCTION IN MASS SOCIETY

By educational production we mean the pedagogical actions that transform students in mind and body, training them to take their places in the adult world. This transformation succeeds when these young children can walk in a line with others, sit in a seat quietly, listen to and obey the instructions of teachers; when they can successfully play out the role and behaviors of the student. It occurs as a result of pedagogic work, wherein teachers use their skills to make children aware of the cultural arbitrary of the school and the language they must master to succeed. Teaching in the earliest grades prepares youth for schoolwork in the upper grades until the student graduates into the work force. This educational knowledge produced through the work of teachers has its counterpart in the demands of the workplace, where the same virtues of punctuality, dependency, and subordination to established authority are so important. The reproduction of the social relations of schools and society have a unity of needs in other advanced capitalist states, as the work of Durkheim, Bourdieu, Althusser, and Mannheim have shown. There is a need to use the same forms of pedagogic work and authority to control the bodily movements of students in mass institutions. There is a need to study those social forces that structure and control pedagogic work in educational systems. Educational production refers to the way youths are transformed into docile, legitimate students by educators working in state schools that demand particular cultural and linguistic requirements of them. This training is meant to prepare students for their life in the productive sector of society and as citizens in a plutocracy that encourages citizens not to think about the inequalities associated with the economic system. Educational production is a way of training children in the ways of cooperation and in the acceptance of the social relations that exist in the schools and society. These educated persons learn the ideology and common beliefs of their families and schools; they learn to explain what is happening to them at home and elsewhere in terms of commonsense understandings of the past. Ideology permeates the schools, causing a clash between the ideas of working-class and poor students and the essentially business-class values and interpretations of educators. This struggle forces youth to accept or reject their roles as ignorant and unworthy students. They must learn about the distortions in such educational production or accept ideas about themselves and their families that are stereotypical and demeaning.

Educational production also refers to the specific ways youth learn to accept the legitimacy and moral understandings of classroom life. This happens when students accept the teachers' right to decide everything that happens in the learning situation and to evaluate students' work on a continuous and arbitrary basis. The final product is one that society demands: a docile worker and unquestioning citizen, who accepts the status quo without question.

This educational production differs from other forms of production because no raw materials are transformed into finished commodities. The finished product will not be available for many years and will require the constant labor of many teachers. The process can be thought of in a way that follows Balibar's work. Certain invariant components seem to exist in every form of educational production known to us. Following Balibar, these can be combined in many ways, as they have been at different times and places in the past. They can be thought of as ideal types: the teacher who does the actual work in the production of educational knowledge; the educational production process, or the pedagogic work and arbitrary habituses that are taught to students; the outcomes of these productive processes, that is, the students' ideas, thoughts, understandings, and emotions; the instruments used in the production process, or those buildings, materials, legitimate knowledge, and organizational structures used to transmit educational knowledge to students; and the higher levels of schooling and work that use educational knowledge for their own purposes in selecting those who are and are not competent to hold certain places in higher education or higher-level occupational positions.

These components of educational production are simply tools that need to be studied in their historical contexts. They cannot be understood without placing them in the social, political, and economic structures of the times. The social relations of material production must be considered as a determining variable in explaining the ways schools organize themselves to train future citizens and workers in different historical eras.

This production of educational knowledge transforms the language children learn in their classrooms. The language of the streets and the home is now proscribed, and a new variation is required. Self-concepts of youngsters also change, along with their view of their parents and their neighborhoods. Curriculum is presented to students as valid knowledge that has been legitimated by the best people in the state and society. These ideological presentations are presented as science, even though they have little to do with the scientific method and rest primarily on the traditions and mores of the more dominant classes in society. History is ignored by these educational transmissions, even as it is taught in some classrooms. The class positions of the historians and the language which they substitute for the social reality they purport to describe distort and change the meaning of what has happened in the distant and recent past. Instruction in state schools presupposes a student who does not know, who needs instruction, and who can learn only the rudiments of educational knowledge and science. The minds of children are to be instructed in the valid culture and mores of the times. This represents the ideological foundations of educational production: societies seek to perpetuate themselves by training new workers and citizens who can carry on their traditions and ways of doing things. Ideology is steeped in the social reality of individuals and exists to guide them in their daily lives. It provides schooling with a powerful way of thinking and understanding the world around it. Because educational systems in modern society are class bound, because their traditions are related to older practices and outside social, economic, and political forces, we must look to these other structures in society if we wish to understand the way that particular school systems are structured.

Since Marx published his studies of mid-nineteenth century capitalism, many organizational and production changes have taken place. The scientific management movement of the early twentieth century led to a consolidation of bureaucratic trends, which are still observable in educational and business systems. The rationalization of work sought to increase the efficiency of workers by simplifying their tasks. Assembly lines were one example of this trend, but the idea permeated all levels of the productive processes. Workers were asked to do the same things over and over again without becoming bored and disinterested, without simply absenting themselves or walking off the job. A new kind or organizational man was needed by these new forms of productive labor, and schooling attempted to train such workers for life in mass industrialized and urban centers.

This simplification of work reduced workers to appendages of machines, to robots or automatons. Their work in state institutions, schools, and business became segmented and increasingly meaningless because of its routine nature. Workers, who had always been thought of as an expensive cost of production, now found themselves working in organizations that saw them as expendable and interchangeable parts of the work process. The meaninglessness of such work was aggravated further by the powerlessness employees experienced in the new bureaucratic environments. Hierarchies were formed and justified by a reference to their higher levels of education, training, experience, and managerial skills. In response to these new demands, schools maintained and deepened their commitment to drill and rote pedagogies, teaching youth to accept meaningless schoolwork as their daily fare. The work was taught in segments, mimicking the new conditions in the workplace. Children found themselves powerless to effect the pedagogic actions of teachers and the harsh disciplinary conditions that were carried over from earlier periods. The authority of teachers to decide every aspect of the classroom situation was justified in ways similar to those used by the emergent managerial classes: they were better educated and trained in the educational sciences, more deserving of their authority than students or their parents.

The powers within the new production and distribution systems of wealth had another aim above and beyond the controlling of surplus value: to reduce labor and its costs, to take from labor its right to control the work in factories and offices. Bureaucracy and the scientific movement spread to state and business organizations during this period with an amazing rapidity. Workers became more interchangeable with one another and less important to the productive processes. The focus of labor strife had always been higher wages, with few labor unions focusing their efforts on the ways surplus values were disposed. The consciousness of workers remained at this trade union level even as they found themselves powerless to affect the ways work was done in increasingly complex industrial organizations. These processes of standardization and simplification had their echo in the schools, where bureaucratic reforms were seen as an improvement over the militaristic schools of the 1870s and 1880s. Yet the schools were no less crowded than they had been, and militaristic, penal, and religious disciplines remained unshaken and unchanged from earlier periods. A pedagogy that was boring, routine, and characterized by an emphasis on drill caused many students to drop out before they finished their elementary educations. Educational training was alienated from the everyday experiences immigrant and urban poor youth were encountering as they sought to assimilate into the American culture. The ideas of individual freedom and worth were contradicted by the strict control of students' movements in school buildings and by their subjection to ridicule and humiliation in competitive classroom situations. Students and their parents remained unaware of the reasons that public schools did not meet the obvious needs of their students, as both workers and the business classes agreed that training for the world of work was an important goal of such institutions. Children living in mean tenement buildings found little of relevance in the curriculum of the schools. The problems of living wages and unionism were almost never discussed there, nor was attention paid to the difficulties immigrant families encountered. The authority structures of schools, the state and business economy were glorified but never challenged by these schools. Millions of people were relocating from different parts of the globe, and yet their experiences were not taken into account by state schools in the United States.

THE IMPORTANCE OF HISTORY

Attempts to include historical evidence in social inquiries of schooling must deal with the cultural, linguistic, and ideological problems inherent in such an approach. Schooling can be studied by focusing on its own inner structures and processes, its own history. But it also needs to be explained as part of a larger totality, a totality which includes the social, economic, and political structures of its surrounding communities. The social relations that develop in the production of material wealth, as one primary example, affect every other form of social relationships that develops in a given society. They affect the way neighborhoods and neighborhood schools are organized, and they also determine a great deal of the cultural and linguistic experiences children will have once they are in the streets or classrooms. It is our view that there is an interaction and mutual influence of social, political, cultural, and economic forces upon one another and upon the schools that reproduce the conditions of their continued existence. Though schooling has presented itself as an unchanging, timeless, and legitimate institution charged with preparing youth for their citizenship roles in society, a struggle has been going on between those who would change it to meet more idealistic, equalitarian goals and those who are comfortable with things as they have been in the past.

Any systematic approach to the study of schooling must seek out the internal-relatedness of the various elements in society, considering the economic, social, political, and cultural as integrated and partially enclosed parts of one social formation. Of course the difficulties such concepts lead to are worrisome: The fragmentation of reality in order to make it more amenable to study and analyses leads to a separation and reification of reality that moves us away from praxis, and this movement away from social reality can lead to confusions and is to be resisted by any means possible.

Still, describing schooling in modern society is difficult. Educational systems are not easy to characterize across national and cultural barriers, even as they all appear to have as their primary purpose the reproduction of the social relations of educational and material production. Ideologies abound in education, yet empiricists claim they can learn what schools are really like by simply observing what happens in classrooms. These pragmatists believe that the relations between teachers and students are at the crux of the problem and that reforms in these relationships will improve the schooling of all youth. Without noting the part that outside forces play in structuring the organizational features of schooling and what is considered legitimate educational knowledge, how well can these researchers know the true conditions in any classroom? When the actors themselves are unaware of the conflictual nature of their associations, when they do not know the unconscious motivations that move them to act as they do, how can the observer know these things? How can the observer understand what is happening when students and teachers are often unaware of the ways in which the interaction between them is structured by outside forces in government? Can observers see the ways in which linguistic and cultural demands operate in the day-to-day work of students and teachers? Can they understand why it is so important to keep voluminous records for many years, records which are used to track and place children? Then there are the problems associated with changing observed interaction into linguistic and coded data. Will observers be aware of the assumptions such methods imply? Can they appreciate that such transformations of data distort their findings significantly? If subjects are interviewed to validate the findings for researchers, can we be sure that such findings are nothing more than what students and teachers felt they ought to say or believed the researcher wanted them to say? There are many other problems between would-be knowers and the students and teachers they wish to observe, which we have discussed in an earlier chapter.

If we assume, then, that it is not possible to convey accurately the real world of classroom life, we must find other means of discourse that can mediate our perceptions and understanding of ongoing practice. These have to be thought of as successive approximations, or approximate knowledge, the best we can hope for in the social and theoretical sciences. An approximate measurement can be made between our perceptual abilities and the objects we wish to perceive, and a succession of further approximations added as we progress in our studies. These are temporary findings, to be scrapped some day when other insights are discovered. Empiricists, of course, believe that observations and theories rooted in provable maxims are sufficient evidential data. Rationalists, on the other hand, have developed abstractions about logical thinking that ensure some correspondence between social reality and their ability to comprehend it.

But rationalism has problems it has not been able to solve successfully. As it often presupposes a correspondence between its concepts and the external world of reality, it does not investigate these presuppositions. Rather, it assumes that they are a development that reflects social reality, determining the way connections are made among things that are perceived and understood in the object world. Logic and rationality are used to include and exclude certain concepts and phenomena, to determine what is and what is not happening or possible in an observed situation. The assumption that humans are rational beings removed from their animal nature does not seem tenable in today's war-torn and chaotic world. Rationalism presupposes that reality is orderly, independent, knowable, and an autonomous force, even though all of these assumptions are unproved and unprovable.

Direct access to reality in classrooms and schools is impossible, as descriptions of observed phenomena must always be in language or signification codes. This means that the representation system needs far greater study and attention than it has received in the pre-Althusserian period. Still, we do not accept ideas that conceive of history as mere myth, not to be taken seriously. Social theory and inquiry needs to pay greater attention to the way such communications from the past are constructed and to the class positions of the writers. It may be that there is a sense in which we can never know social reality, that we can never move outside our own stereotypes, prejudices, and linguistic concepts of the mind. But we can take these distorting elements into account when we do our work. What we see, how we see it, and what we make of our observations of classroom life need to be stated in conditional terms, and some effort has to be made to read the unconscious messages transmitted from one generation to the next. The real world may be difficult to access, but human beings have some facility here.

The point is that our consciousness can be raised by sociocultural theories of schooling even as we reject certain parts of them. History can be read in more critical ways; it can help us to differentiate between what was believed in the past in a commonsense way and the ways these ideological effects influenced the lives of those who worked and studied in those times. There is a separation between our ability to understand and our ability to convey the social world to others, as Kant noted many years ago. But we can understand and convey in such a way that makes conclusions tentative and knowledge gained from such studies approximations that will be changed some day when we learn more about ourselves and the world we live in.

A sociocultural theory of totality, examining the many features of modern society as attributes that coexist and influence one another, seems a viable mode of analysis and interpretation for future work in these areas. Such ideas have their beginnings in Hegelian philosophy and are meant to convey a harmony between the opposed and contradictory forces in modern society. The thrust of these concepts is that features of social formations are not isolated. They do not include only conflict or only harmonious behaviors by individuals. Rather, they are inseparable from one another and cannot be separated for analytical purposes, either. The social relations of production influence such relations in educational systems and are in turn affected by the pedagogic practices of schools. Both economic and educational institutions cannot be separated without doing damage to the social relations and reality that develop between workers and managers and students and teachers. A change in the way a teacher teaches leads inevitably to a change in the learning processes of children. New levels of learning will change the social relations between them, encouraging the teacher to seek even more effective methods of instruction. Teachers and students interact, establishing relations that further influence how learning situations are structured. They act and react to one another, creating a total or organizational entity known as classroom life; and they do this even though they are unconscious of many of their motivations, even though they are unaware and insufficiently concerned with the social forces outside the classroom that structure, in the final instance, what actually happens to them each school day.

The idea that social institutions and phenomena should be seen as part of a totality introduces the concept and problems associated with mediation. Mediation suggests a method that allows for the identification and intercession of opposing or adversarial parts of the schooling or economic system under examination. By mediation is meant something other than the empiricist's use of the word, wherein educational production is merely a reflection of the economic and social needs of a particular society. This usage assumes that education, religion, philosophy, and science are reflections of a material world that influences but is not influenced by them. The social, political, cultural, and educational parts of a social system are seen as passive, having little effect on the economic structures that support them. Here differences between ideological and scientific effects come into play, with the latter attempting to provide real knowledge while the former distorts the world in which people live.

The idea of mediation is different from reflective theories and doctrines. It attempts to avoid fragmenting social reality by analyzing phenomena as a complex of reciprocal relations that create and reproduce their own structures and reality. The methods of schooling can no longer be seen in isolation, separate from the economy and society they serve. Schooling must be viewed as an integral part of this totality that they seek to reproduce again and again. Accordingly, no part of classroom life can be studied without relating it to the total social system it serves, without paying attention to the class structure that exists in the adult world. Every classroom relationship is now seen to enter every other relationship in the school and society, and the outcomes of schooling are linked more firmly to other features of the cultural life around it.

Because schooling's ties to the economic sector and social mores of a society are so great, educational production needs to be studied with these determining influences in mind; each must be studied to learn how they influence and are influenced by one another. Streaming, grading, selecting, stigmatizing slow learners, and the rest are not pedagogically sound practices. They can only be understood when linked to the kind of social relations that exist in the workplace and social world of adults, when they assume their places in the social system's efforts to reproduce its economic and social relations.

Notes

CHAPTER 1

1. Louis Althusser, *For Marx*, trans. B. Brewster (London: New Left Books, 1969), 85.

2. Pierre Bourdieu, *Reproduction in Education, Society and Culture* (Beverly Hills, Calif.: Sage Publications, 1977).

3. Ted Benton, *The Rise and Fall of Structural Marxism* (New York: St. Martin's Press, 1984), 98-104.

4. Paul Hirst, "Althusser and the Theory of Ideology," *Economy and Society*, 5, no. 4 (November 1980): 385-412.

5. R. Geuss, *The Idea of Critical Theory* (Cambridge: Cambridge University Press, 1981), Ch. 1.

6. Karl Marx, *The German Ideology* (London: Lawrence and Wishart, 1958), 67.

7. Karl Mannheim, *Ideology and Utopia* (New York: Harcourt, Brace & World, Inc., 1936).

8. S. Smith. *Reading Althusser: An Essay on Structural Marxism* (Ithaca: Cornell University Press, 1984), 106-8.

9. Basil Bernstein, *The Structuring of Pedagogic Discourse*, vol. 4 (London: Routledge, 1990), 134-36.

10. Ibid., 140-42.

11. V. J. Seidler, et al. *One-Dimensional Marxism* (London: Allison & Busby, 1980), 133-39.

CHAPTER 2

1. Erich Fromm, *Marx's Concept of Man* (New York: Frederick Ungar Publishing Co., 1969), 169-96.

2. Ralph Miliband, "Marx and the State." In *The Socialist Register 1965*, ed. R. Miliband and J. Saville (New York: Monthly Review Press, 1965), 279-80.

3. Karl Marx and Friedrich Engels, *Selected Works*, 2 vols. (Moscow: Foreign Language Publishers, 1958), 37-39.

4. Miliband, "Marx and the State," 280-86.

5. Ted Benton, *The Rise and Fall of Structural Marxism* (New York: St. Martin's Press, 1984), 143-50.

6. Ellwood P. Cubberley, *The History of Education* (Cambridge, Mass.: Houghton-Mifflin Company, 1920), 671-72.

7. David B. Tyack, *Turning Points in American History* (Waltham, Mass.: Blaisdell Publishing Company, 1967), 14-17.

8. Michael Katz, *School Reform: Past and Present* (Boston, Mass.: Little, Brown and Company, 1971), 43-48.

9. David Nasaw, *Schooled to Order* (New York: Oxford University Press, 1979), 81-82.

10. Katz, *School Reform*, 151-52.

11. David Rothman, *The Discovery of the Asylum* (Boston, Mass.: Little, Brown and Co. (1971), 262-63.

12. Stanley K. Schultz, *The Culture Factory* (New York: Oxford University Press, 1973), 298-300.

13. Elwood P. Cubberley, *Public Education in the United States* (Boston, Mass.: Houghton-Mifflin Company, 1934), 480-84.

14. Irving Howe, *World of Our Fathers* (New York: Simon and Schuster, 1976), 272-74.

15. Colin Greer, *The Great School Legend* (New York: Basic Books, 1972), 19-20.

16. Ibid, 105-29.

17. Ibid, 116-17.

18. Lawrence A. Cremin, *The Transformation of the School: Progressivism in American Education: 1867-1957* (New York: Random House, Vintage Books, 1964), 3-22.

19. Harry Braverman, *Labor and Monopoly Capital: The Degradation of Work in the Twentieth Century* (New York: Monthly Review Press, 1974), 284-89.

20. Nasaw, *Schooled to Order*, 173-83.

21. Ibid., 177-78.

22. Steven B. Smith, *Reading Althusser: An Essay on Structural Marxism* (Ithaca: Cornell University Press, 1984), 149-50.

23. Karl Marx, *Grundisse, Foundations of the Critique of Political Economy (1857-58)*, trans. Martin Nicolaus (Harmondsworth: Penguin Books, 1973), 99-103.

CHAPTER 3

1. Pierre Bourdieu and J. C. Passeron, *Reproduction in Education, Society and Culture* (Beverly Hills, Calif.: Sage Publications, 1977), 54-67.

2. Ibid., 4-7.

3. Pierre Bourdieu, *The Inheritors: French Students and Their Relation to Culture* (Chicago: University of Chicago Press, 1979), 3-12.

4. Bourdieu and Passeron, *Reproduction in Education*, 31-35.

5. Bourdieu, *The Inheritors*, 1-28.

6. Bourdieu and Passeron, *Reproduction in Education*, 73.

7. Ibid., 73-74.

8. Ibid., 35-37.

9. Stanley W. Rothstein, "The Ethics of Coercion." *Urban Education* 22, no. 1 (April 1987): 53-72.

10. Bourdieu and Passeron, *Reproduction in Education*, 54-67.

11. Emile Durkheim, *Education and Sociology* (New York: Free Press, 1956).

12. Louis Althusser, *For Marx*, trans. Ben Brewster (London: Allen Lane, Penguin Press, 1972), 85.

13. Ted Benton, *The Rise and Fall of Structured Marxism* (New York: St. Martin's Press, 1984), 152-53.

14. Bourdieu and Passeron, *Reproduction in Education*, 4-7.

CHAPTER 4

1. Ted Benton, *The Rise and Fall of Structural Marxism* (New York: St. Martin's Press, 1984), 11-14.

2. S. Smith, *Reading Althusser* (Ithaca: Cornell University Press, 1984), 176-78.

3. Benton, *Structural Marxism*, 12-13.

4. J. Lacan, "The Function of Language in Psychoanalysis." In W. E. Steinkraus, *The Language of the Self*, ed. (Baltimore: University Press of Johns Hopkins, 1968), 39.

5. K. McDonnell and K. Robins, S. Clarke, V. J. Seidler, and T. Lovell, *One Dimensional Marxism* (London: Allison & Busby, 1980), 197-99.

6. Lacan, "Function of Language," 39-41.

7. R. A. Spitz, *The First Years of Life* (New York: International Press, 1965), 94-95.

8. McDonnell, Robins et al., *One Dimensional Marxism*, 12.

9. E. Kris, "The Recovery of Childhood Memories in Psychoanalysis." In *The Psychoanalytic Study of the Child* (New York: International Universities Press, 1956), 76.

10. G. Blanck and R. Blanck, *Ego Psychology: Theory and Practice* (New York: Columbia University Press, 1974), 53-60.

11. G. Simmel, *The Sociology of Georg Simmel* (New York: Free Press, 1950), 385-87.

12. L. Althusser, *For Marx*, trans. Ben Brewster (London: Allen Lane, Penguin Press, 1969), 229-36.

13. L. Althusser, *Reading Capital*, trans. Ben Brewster (London: New Left Books, 1970), 32-34.

14. L. Althusser, *Lenin and Other Essays*, trans. Ben Brewster (London: New Left Books, 1971), 121-73.

15. A. Schutz, *Collected Papers*, vol. 1 (The Hague: Martinus Nijhoff, 1962).

16. *One Dimensional Marxism*, 241-42.

CHAPTER 5

1. Ted Benton, *The Rise of Structural Marxism* (New York: St. Martin's Press, 1984), 68-69.

2. E. Fromm, *Marx's Concept of Man* (New York: Frederick Ungar Publishing Co., 1961), 176.

3. Ibid., 110.

4. Paul Sweezy, *The Theory of Capitalist Development* (New York: Oxford University Press, 1942), 59-62.

5. Karl Marx, *Capital: A Critique of Political Economy* (New York: The Modern Library, Random House, 1906), 57, 185.

6. Ibid., 834-85.

7. L. Althusser, *Reading Capital*, trans. Ben Brewster (London: New Left Books, 1970), 199-308.

8. S. Clarke, T. Lovell, K. McDonnell, K. Robins, and V. J. Seidler, *One-Dimensional Man* (London: Allison & Busby, 1980), 56-58.

9. Oliver C. Cox, *Caste, Class and Race: A Study in Social Dynamics* (New York: Modern Reader Paperbacks, 1970), 485-86.

10. Benton, *The Rise and Fall of Structural Marxism*, 71-72.

11. Marx, *Capital*, 585-88.

12. Althusser, *Reading Capital*, 214-15.

13. Ted Benton, *The Rise and Fall of Structural Marxism*, 115-18.

14. Ferdinand Tonnies, *Community & Society* (New York: Harper & Row Publishers, 1957), 258-59.

15. Ibid., 1-11.

16. Ibid., 38-40.

17. F. Pappenheim, *The Alienation of Modern Man* (New York: Monthly Review Press, 1959), 74.

18. Tonnies, *Community & Society*, 240-42.

19. Pappenheim, *The Alienation of Modern Man*, 74-75.

20. Tonnies, *Community & Society*, 247.

21. E. Josephson, and M. Josephson, *Man Alone: Alienation in Modern Society* (New York: Dell Publishing, 1961), 86-91.

22. David Tyack, *Turning Points in American Educational History* (Waltham, Mass.: Blaisdell Publishing Co., 1967), 355-57.

23. Cox, *Caste, Class and Race*, 484-86.

CHAPTER 6

1. Basil Bernstein, *Theoretical Studies towards a Sociology of Language. Vol. 1, Class, Codes and Control* (London: Routledge & Kegan Paul, 1975), 121-17.

2. S. Smith, *Reading Althusser: An Essay on Structural Marxism* (Ithaca: Cornell University Press, 1984), 176-78.

3. W. Waller, *The Sociology of Teaching* (New York: Russell & Russell, 1961), 391-92.

4. Oliver C. Cox, *Caste, Class & Race: A Study in Social Dynamics* (New York: Modern Reader Paperbacks, 1970), 545-47.

CHAPTER 7

1. I. Katznelson and M. Weir, *Schooling for All: Class, Race, and the Decline of the Democratic Ideal* (New York: Basic Books, 1985), 20-22; 46-51.

2. S. Bowles and H. Gintis, *Schooling in Capitalist America* (New York: Basic Books, 1976), 53-55.

3. S. Smith, *Reading Althusser: An Essay on Structural Marxism* (Ithaca: Cornell University Press, 1984).

Selected Bibliography

Althusser, Louis. *For Marx*. Translated by Ben Brewster. London: Allen Lane, Penguin Press, 1972.
——— . *Lenin and Other Essays*. Translated by Ben Brewster. London: New Left Books, 1971.
Benton, Ted. *The Rise and Fall of Structural Marxism*. New York: St. Martin's Press, 1984.
Bernstein, Basil. *The Structuring of Pedagogic Discourse*, vol. 4. London: Routledge, 1990.
Blanck, G., and R. Blanck. *Ego Psychology: Theory and Practice*. New York: Columbia University Press, 1974.
Bourdieu, Pierre. *The Inheritors: French Students and Their Relation to Culture*. Chicago: University of Chicago Press, 1979.
Bourdieu, Pierre, and J. C. Passeron. *Reproduction in Education, Society and Culture*. Beverly Hills, Calif.: Sage Publications, 1977.
Bowles, S., and H. Gintis. *Schooling in Capitalist America*. New York: Basic Books, 1976.
Braverman, Harry. *Labor and Monopoly Capital: The Degradation of Work in the Twentieth Century*. New York: Monthly Review Press, 1974.
Cox, O. C. *Caste, Class and Race*. New York: Modern Reader Paperbacks, 1959.
Cremin, Lawrence A. *The Transformation of the School: Progressivism in American Education. 1867-1957*. New York: Random House, Vintage Books, 1964.
Cubberley, Ellwood P. *The History of Education*. Cambridge, Mass.: Houghton-Mifflin Company, 1920.
——— . *Public Education in the United States*. Boston, Mass.: Houghton-Mifflin Company, 1934.
Durkheim, Emile. *Education and Sociology*. New York: Free Press, 1956.
Fromm, E. *Marx's Concept of Man*. New York: Frederick Ungar Publishing Co., 1961.
Geuss, R. *The Idea of Critical Theory*. Cambridge: Cambridge University Press, 1981.

Greer, Colin. *The Great School Legend*. New York: Basic Books, 1972.

Hirst, Paul. "Althusser and the Theory of Ideology." In *Economy and Society*, vol. 5, no. 4. (November 1976).

Howe, Irving. *World of Our Fathers*. New York: Simon and Schuster, 1976.

Josephson, E., and M. Josephson. *Man Alone: Alienation in Modern Society*. New York: Dell Publishing, 1961.

Katz, Michael. *School Reform Past and Present*. Boston, Mass.: Little, Brown and Co., 1971.

Katznelson, I., and M. Weir. *Schooling for All: Class, Race, and the Decline of the Democratic Ideal*. New York: Basic Books, 1985.

Kris, E. "The Recovery of Childhood Memories in Psychoanalysis." In *The Psychoanalytic Study of the Child*. New York: International Universities Press, 1956.

Lacan, J. "The Function of Language in Psychoanalysis." In *The Language of the Self*. Edited by W. E. Steinkraus. Baltimore: Johns Hopkins University Press, 1968.

Mannheim, Karl. *Ideology and Utopia*. New York: Harcourt, Brace & World, Inc., 1936.

Marx, Karl. *Capital: A Critique of Political Economy*. New York: The Modern Library, Random House, 1906.

——— . *Grundisse, Foundations of the Critique of Political Economy (1857-58)*. Translated by Martin Nicolaus. Harmondsworth: Penguin Books, 1973.

Marx, Karl, and Friedrich Engels. *Selected Works*. 2 vols. Moscow: Foreign Language Publishers, 1958.

McDonnell, K., and K. Robins, S. Clarke, V. J. Seidler, and T. Lovell. *One Dimensional Marxism*. London: Allison & Busby, 1980.

Miliband, Ralph. "Marx and the State." In *The Socialist Register 1965*. Edited by R. Miliband, and J. Saville. New York: Monthly Review Press, 1965.

Nasaw, David. *Schooled to Order*. New York: Oxford University Press, 1979.

Pappenheim, F. *The Alienation of Modern Man*. New York: Monthly Review Press, 1959.

Rothman, David. *The Discovery of the Asylum*. Boston, Mass.: Little, Brown and Co., 1971.

Rothstein, Stanley W. "The Ethics of Coercion." *Urban Education* 22, no. 1 (April 1987).

Schultz, Stanley K. *The Culture Factory*. New York: Oxford University Press, 1973.

Schutz, A. *Collected Papers*, vol. 1. The Hague: Martinus Nijhoff, 1962.

Simmel, G. *The Sociology of Georg Simmel*. New York: Free Press, 1950.

Smith, Steven B. *Reading Althusser: An Essay on Structural Marxism*. Ithaca: Cornell University Press, 1984.

Spitz, R. A. *The First Year of Life*. New York: International Press, 1965.

Sweezy, Paul. *The Theory of Capitalist Development*. New York: Oxford University Press, 1942.

Tonnies, Ferdinand. *Community & Society*. New York: Harper & Row, Publishers, 1957.

Tyack, David B. *Turning Points in American History*. Waltham, Mass.: Blaisdell Publishing Company, 1967.

Waller, W. *The Sociology of Teaching*. New York: Russell & Russell, 1961.

Index

About the Author

STANLEY WILLIAM ROTHSTEIN is Professor of Education at California State University, Fullerton. He is especially interested in the sociology of education, and he brings to his work several years of experience as a teacher and administrator in the New York City school system. He has published several books and numerous articles on urban education and sociology.